Dear Susan,
Great to walk
this path with you,
Joe

The Truth in Twenty
... and Then Some

Entries from my journal / a rolling memoir

Joe Wise

BALBOA
PRESS

A DIVISION OF HAY HOUSE

Balboa Press books may be ordered through booksellers or by contacting:

Balboa Press
A Division of Hay House
1663 Liberty Drive
Bloomington, IN 47403
www.balboapress.com
1-(877) 407-4847

Because of the dynamic nature of the Internet, any web addresses or links contained in this book may have changed since publication and may no longer be valid. The views expressed in this work are solely those of the author and do not necessarily reflect the views of the publisher, and the publisher hereby disclaims any responsibility for them.

The author of this book does not dispense medical advice or prescribe the use of any technique as a form of treatment for physical, emotional, or medical problems without the advice of a physician, either directly or indirectly. The intent of the author is only to offer information of a general nature to help you in your quest for emotional and spiritual well-being. In the event you use any of the information in this book for yourself, which is your constitutional right, the author and the publisher assume no responsibility for your actions.

Front cover photos and design elements by Maleita Wise

Printed in the United States of America.

ISBN: 978-1-4525-8109-5 (sc)
ISBN: 978-1-4525-8110-1 (e)

Balboa Press rev. date: 9/6/2013

Contents

They seek the truth, before they can die

Crosby, Stills and Nash
"Teach Your Children"

to Maleita,
      my truest, clearest
      mirror
and Bruce,
      the great, good
         gift of him.

Gratitude

I keep a gratitude journal by my bed. Every night I write down, in a few words, six "things" (people, experiences, events) from this day I am grateful for. Maleita does too. Sometimes one of us will look at the other and say, "This may take a while." They do always come. Most days I have more than six, but I stop there. Leaving me flush with unmeasured bounty. I am more and more impressed by how small these things are (someone held a door for me, looked at me when they handed me my change, called me with something "dumb" they had done) and how large are their prints on my grateful heart.

Most days' entries for me include the sound of someone's voice, the connection, that we *can* connect, and *do*. I'll just *write*, "Talked to Eric."

I am writing this piece in lieu of the list of thank yous I see in almost every book. My life has been, is being, blessed by many friends, and many people. Some are in this book. *All* are gift.

The one name arising *here*, in great gratitude, is Sandy Tillotson, who has been on this book "marathon" from the starting line, helping me format this collection, even as we re-format our lives.

Thanks, Sandy.

Foreword

The Truth in Twenty. The twenty is minutes. Many of the pieces in this collection were born in that span. Most, entries from my journal.

I'm not sure I've personally seen a book in quite this category—or a category for this book. Not easy to corral. It's the "And Then Some" that adds the wild mustangs. And more minutes. Many pieces were specifically encouraged by friends. Part memoir, part spiritual, part kissing the everyday, part history, part self revelation. But done in "pieces." The experiences that stood out for me. Thus far.

Blessedly, I had many to choose from. Some will wait for other books.

My deepest hope is that you will see yourself in these "visits," these pieces, these expressions. And be moved to find and share your own. In *your* medium. In your *life*.

Intro to the Intro

Every major change in my interior life has manifested itself as Something inside of me taking one big giant step and then the rest of me "catching up."

This book mirrors that pattern. My intro was ready in 2004. The rest of the book has been "catching up." Morphing considerably along the way. In form. And content.

Until it was content.

Please consider yourself introduced to the introduction.

Intro

I'm going to see what writing an intro to my book is like by going about it the same way I've done most of the book. Timed writing. Usually 20 to 25 minutes.

I've been in a journal group for seven years, almost as long as I've lived in Sedona. We take turns giving topics. We all write for about 20, then have the option of sharing. The members of my group have encouraged me to publish some of my entries.[1] Encouragement.

Hesitations. Will it be too personal? Too many clothes off? Will it offend family members who may be indirectly included? Who saw and reacted to events differently? Will it be too guarded in the age of blogs, live journals, and reality shows? Not juicy enough? I want to be brave but not foolhardy. Relevant. Read. Admired. I am now in the land of least control.

The Truth in Twenty is catchy I hope. *Writing into Your Life* was my "almost" choice. Like diving into your life, your accumulated experiences to discover, usually for the first time consciously, the truth or meaning abiding there. Writing *into* your life, not *about* it—though the distance of fair witness that happens in "about" is significant. My best "entries" have all been beginning with no clear idea where I might go, and trusting my hand, to transcribe the emerging path of my mind and heart. I've always liked the use of the word "entry" for keeping a journal, and have it keep you. A little like Alice going through the door. To my own interior. Some things familiar. Some not. Some comforting. Some disturbing.

Turning on the lights. Embracing the dark. Finding release and relief. Confronting. Accepting. Clarity. Peace.

It seems kind of funny to me to be a writer most of my life, and not come to the journal table till age 45. I certainly had amassed enough to chew on.

It was great to be in a place where grammar, compound sentences, rhyme schemes, spelling and even making sense were not only not required, but even not useful.

At 45, twenty years ago now, I discovered I was pretty much a mature American male (for better or worse) in every dimension of my life, save for my emotional self. I had also managed to reach that age, thanks to a wonderful relationship and an engaging, fulfilling career in music and teaching, without any significant foray into my early life. My upbringing. My family dynamic.

I quickly learned my most satisfying and fruitful entries related to how I felt. With less and less reference to expectation. Others, or my own. Emotional truth. The most precious and difficult-to-harvest pearl, subject as it is, to the fear of not belonging.

Standing in my own truth, feeling disloyal to many I loved/love, I took many big blind leaps inside. I have done some physically brave things. None felt as courageous as this trek.

I now pass on ways to enter this process in workshops and classrooms, and in an ongoing way at an addictions treatment center in Sedona.

It would be my hope that you might read this book, and put it down, and start your own. Without an eye for publishing. For your eyes only, as all truth writing begins with me. When I teach a teen this process, I think of it as an alternative to drugs, crime and Columbine. I feel safer in a world whose members lead an examined life, express their feelings.

I wish it was required at the point of sale for guns. Criminal, citizen, policeman. I feel much more comfortable in the presence of the ones who keep a journal, looking for their own truth, finding a way to rage without hurting themselves or anybody else,[2] embracing our own uniqueness and sameness, blessing our place in the world. No less than the trees and the stars.

Well, there's my intro. Not perfect. I like it. Perfect would be a good word to let go of. And there's twenty minutes.

Meditation

Here is a meditation I enter into before I open my journal to make an entry. Unless I'm too distraught or agitated to have any hope of arriving at stillness. I have honed this down over the years to all the ingredients I need to orient myself. If you resonate with it, you might record it and have your own voice guide you into center. The three dots are for pauses, silence.

Begin with a couple of deep breaths...

Pay particular attention to letting go of *all* the air...

Trusting the Universe to give it back...

Noticing the more I release, the more I receive...

Relaxing on the in-betweens...

Aware for a moment of this silent grace full contract I have with the Universe I ordinarily need pay no attention to...

I breathe Life; Life breathes me...

And I begin to let go of everything that came before *this* moment...

If a thought or feeling arises, an outside noise presents itself, I don't resist it, I just let it float by, like a cloud in the sky...

There is no need to hold on to anything...

There is nothing to prove, nothing to plan...

And I begin to let go of my image of myself...

(I may notice some feelings of fear, I may notice some feelings of *relief*...)[3]

I let go of my image of myself as I think others *might* see me...

This, that remains, This, that never leaves, This, that is never separate from the Divine, This, my true Self,

I rest here...

(longest "pause" or opportunity to experience stillness)

And as I am ready, I open my eyes in this room.

A Meditation on the Meditation

I don't remember whether it was Ty Cobb, or Yogi Berra, or neither who said, when asked how to steal a base, "First, you have to leave the one you're on." It's that way for breathing, perhaps our best primal reminder, of life here being loss and recovery, surrender and discovery. We lose our breath every few seconds. Complete exhalation opens me to fuller readiness and capacity for oxygen-rich bounty.

I let go of everything that came before *this* moment. Another doorway into living in the now. Resisting the "pop ups" usually gives them more strength and longer "presence." They're like incoming calls, while I'm already connected and in communion/conversation with my still self. I can take the call or call them back or neither. I keep a notepad by me in case something really, really big pops up. I write it down. Let it go. Till after this process. For now, clouds floating by.

I let go of my image of myself. The first few times for this can be scary. What am I, if not a father, a provider, a husband, a singer? Is there any "substance" to me without these? Do I exist? What if all my years of fidelity, and care, and enhancing my reputation went out the window? I was in a steam room with strangers? A human being, not a human doing. At the first hint of my openness to this, I am flooded with relief. Scare is "getting there." Getting there is relief. It allows me the experience to resonate with Rumi's announcement: "the soul is here for its own joy."

This, that remains, never leaves, is never separate from the

Divine. The Eastern mystics have long counseled us to look for that which does not come and go. For me it invariably comes back to that nameless, formless, consciousness and presence I experience as the "I" of my being. My seat of awareness. Awareness itself. It acknowledges a sometimes *sense* of separation from the Divine. It *experiences no separation*. It is my forever safe place, though I choose to "come and go" from it. For now, it is chosen home, bliss, center, at–easement. Content.[4]

Keeping a Journal

A journal, I've discovered, means lots of things to lots of people. For me it has become a place to be intimate with myself. A process that encourages "awakened awareness" as Catherine Ingram calls it. An invitation to tell myself the truth, especially about how I feel and what I want and why.

I am not aware of any time I've lied to myself with a pen in my hand. With it, I have discovered I often have more than one feeling at a time; the second and third are usually not noble. Nor are most of the second and third "hidden" *motivations*. The most frequent of these is revenge. This must be why I gravitate to so many movies and stories that feature this gem of a gratifier. Justice, fairness, and retribution without the lofty demands of forgiveness. Makes my world feel safer, cleaner, neater. Then again, this is the core script for century after century of war, and perhaps many bumpy karmic returns.

Yet without my acknowledgement of the dark feelings and shadow desires and drives in myself, and you in yours, I hold no hope for a better world. Forgiveness, the relief of it, not brought on by the "rightness" of it, but by finding myself in positions much like those before or around me whom I cursed, and feeling and knowing how easy it is to act out of a fear I couldn't admit even if I could name. How powerful a drive it is to survive—physically, emotionally, fiscally, spiritually. How outrageous it is for me to die or be enslaved in some manner while you throw away your leftovers. It's enough to drive a man or a woman to extreme behaviors.

Gandhi, Mandela, Martin Luther King took a different path.

A mother came to Gandhi and said, "Tell my child to stop eating sugar." Gandhi said, "Bring him back in two weeks." She came. Gandhi looked at her son and told him to quit eating sugar. The woman said, "Why didn't you tell him that two weeks ago?" He answered, "Two weeks ago I had not stopped eating sugar." Entering the experience through the "same" human gate. Owning the feeling, choosing not to act out of it. Willing to acknowledge the dark and the capacity for hate and violence while at the same time electing to talk, protest, march, be loud and persistent.

I've taken more time on this dimension of journaling than I expected. It is more core to me than I thought.

I like the surprise of journaling that emphasizes personal clarity, release, insight and surprise. I think of it as writing into my life, like diving into my life—to see what mysteries lie there, may unfold there. Much like Greg Louganis, my favorite diver of all time, I have done this many times. Yet each time, once I leave the board, or pick up my pen, anything can happen. I am still a mystery to me, you are still a mystery to me, as is the world.

I cut out, tear out, or save some images that I feel a connection with. I put them in a big envelope I paste inside the back cover of my journal. Pictures from nature, portraits, ticket stubs, post cards, art invitations. On a day when I want to look inside myself through this process and I do not have some issue or event "up" for me or prodding me, I pick out one of these images or items, paste it on my next blank page, pick up my pen, and *discover* what my connection with it is, let it reveal why I saved it in the first place.

On the other inside back panel of my journal, I paste a smaller envelope with small pieces of paper I've written a "topic" on when it came to me. It finds its way first into my wallet, then to this envelope. These are often questions, lists, or what I call "dot-dot-dot phrases." The truth is… Bliss is… I felt afraid when… I want to be admired when I… things I can revisit many times, as in "you can't cross the same river twice." Lists are especially fruitful. They render so many topics. One of my favorites has been: Name five things in my life I've consistently run from and five things I've stopped and turned and faced into. My goal is to get them on the same list. Maybe in *this* lifetime. Name five times (I like five but if my pen wants to keep going, I let it) I did a brave thing. If I can't yet give myself the accolade—five times I did a *hard* thing.

Questions, as a source for topics or diving boards, were my first stimulus for entries. I had so many of them that I wanted to ask my parents. I, in my 40's ready to ask them; they, having died in my 30's. After some period of frustration with their unavailability, a light went on. These would be *great* questions to ask *yourself*. The first one I wanted to ask my Dad. "How did your parents punish you and how do you think that affected your life after that?" It was close to the first entry I wrote in a journal. It was almost certainly the first entry that revealed to me there was a way out of my prisons. This smaller envelope serves the way my picture one does on I-want-to-connect-with-myself-but-have-no-current-issue days.

I don't write in my journal every day. I've met so many people who assume big-time guilt over not being "faithful" to their journaling experience. It often becomes *the* reason for avoidance. It may end up not being a useful tool for you. But if it is, I invite you to not give it up just because you took a five-year break. My guess is the guilt or shame comes from not doing *anything* to stay in communion with ourselves. We miss the connection, and our psycho/ eco system feels out of whack. Often we are fully engaged in *having* an experience and the time to process it will come later. Whatever the "reason," it becomes another opportunity to treat ourselves with compassion. I have set as my main goal in life to become fully self-compassionate. I am banking on this taking care of everything else. And my relationship with everything else. I do know when I am in the presence of someone who is at ease with himself, with herself, I can be tended to without a word, I am received as fully as I receive myself. Sometimes more. My feet are washed, with no pan.

Whatever we do to put ourselves in either position, I believe, is of the highest of world work. Even, and maybe especially, the solitary, unaudienced gift of sitting ourselves down with a full pen and empty paper to meet our selves.

Karen and Elliott. Before the Names.

"Be as you are," Ramana Maharshi says. Before naming and clothing. Before the mind, wonderful as it is, clouds over our splendor.

When Karen, my niece, delivered her first child, I was glad to go visit. She was relaxed, tiredly joyful, all but glowing. It was a peaceful maternity ward. Maleita, her aunt by family, and mother of our two children, with me pulled two chairs up close to Karen's bed. We shared, basked really, in the event that truly silences us all.

After a while a nurse told the new mom her baby was on the way for feeding. Maleita and I moved our chairs back to the wall and watched in silence as this new fresh-skinned one arrived on wheels and was parked right next to his mother's bed. The nurse left wordlessly and for the next minutes, before nursing, the two of them at eye level in their beds, held each other in their gaze. The silence was full.

Then softly, Karen spoke: "Who are you?"

I don't think I've ever heard a better way to start a relationship. Or nurture one. What a gift. To empower this little "helpless" one from the beginning. To open herself to his openings. His surprises. His revelations.

It made me wonder how I might have answered her, or *my* mom, if I had had the words and been asked. To give myself a voice at this, in terms of a lifetime, monumental moment.

It is and has been the finest of tools in self inquiry at any age: "Who am I?" I added, "and how would I like to be raised?" and have written into this several times. Here, following, are two.

Who Am I? How Would I Like to be Raised?

"We are all made of stars… No one can stop us now…" [5]

I am the stuff of stars in body. Undividable divinity in soul. You know me and you don't. I bring unique reflections of what it is to be human. What it is to be Divine.

Look at me. Notice me. Re-spect. Re-look at me. Give me a second and third look, and fourth. Don't give me the onceover. I'll be looking at you and everything around me long, hard and often. Checking out the new. Is it, are you, friendly to my existence? Is it, are you, not? I will base my picture of the universe for better or for worse largely on how you are with me, how you are with you. This picture will last for years, one way or the other.

Ask me who I am often. Allow me to *know*, especially early on when I'm so close to my time with the Divine. And not to know as I get further into the human journey. Teach me things mostly by what you do. This will happen whether you want it to or not. Just be conscious of it, for a quicker more permanent take.

Allow me to miss the mark, fail, and whatever other word you use to describe my not performing as you wish. If it's an important lesson for me—please keep looking for the way I learn. Sometimes visual—sometimes experiential—probably always in conjunction with your example.

Talk across to me, not down to me. If my vocabulary is small, there is no need to put your version of a baby tone in your voice. Save that for our games. Anything shy of this will make it difficult for me to transition and grow. To not think of the world's population as a group of equals—cooperating. The talk down suggests dominance and submission. Smarter and dumber. Powerful and weak. I am fresh from communion with the Divine, so I know this is not true now—but it'll be harder to remember unless you reinforce the Truth of Being.

Let me learn a lot by doing. Teach me early, often, and intently about the biggies that can end or greatly alter my human life— traffic, fire, electricity, gravity. Other than that—let me make my mistakes, flounder, fall, skin up my knees, wield my own crayons, relate freely, resist smothering kisses from Aunt Hannah, stack my own blocks, like my own friends. Intervene when you think my life is in peril, not when I'm making a choice you wouldn't make.

Ask me if I want a suggestion. If it's not a life-threatening situation—go by my reply. Let me discover for me—things you already know. Don't tell me ahead of time what I'll like and not like—don't tell me the end of the movie. Let us be surprised together about how I turn out. Remember I'm always a work, and a play, in progress.

Great to have you as my companion. Thanks for giving me so much energy and attention. I look forward to what we'll share and learn together. I will bless our silences.

Who Am I? How Would I Like to be Raised? II

I am a vivid expression and expressor of what is beyond and in and around matter. I am keenly particle and wave—richly endowed with properties for reflecting the Divine, "shining forth like shook foil."[6]

I am known and unknown. Hoped for and given. Powerless in my current form—needing no power in its soul—my soul—me— needing no power to stand over and against—a fellow star, content in its beingness. Milk—I need it. Milky Way—I *am* it. It is a delicate balance to you—not to me—as I get further along, I may cloud over like you—and forget. For now I am clean and clear about who I am and who you are. Last lifetime we could easily have been reversed. I'm just forgetting that now. I have taken on this body and this life—to experience earth and humanness—to feel, to smell, to taste. These things come and go—*I* do not.

I would like to be raised with love—let me see that above all else. Especially let me see your love for yourself. It will outshine and crowd out every other teaching. Let me see how reverently you deal with other stars who have this mud on them. Reinforce for me this vision we are all in this incarnation experience together. Much of it looks scary. It will be the highest gift to be companioned. Companioned, not lectured or constrained or forced. Do whatever to teach me about trucks in the street, fire on the range, and sparks in the outlets—but all the rest leave me lots of room to learn—to gain my own knowledge and awareness of the truth—slowly if I need. With missteps if I need. I ask you to let go of your embarrassment with me. If it arises, and it will—recognize it. Tell me if you get caught up in it. Don't process *everything* with me. Do that with other big people. But don't hide your feelings from me. If I don't see fear, I won't know it's okay. If I don't see sad, I'll think I'm strange when it comes.

Do whatever you need to be comfortable in your *own* skin—this is the primary prescription for a *relaxed* me. When I see you celebrate differences instead of criticize them, or fear them, or both— I will be in good potting soil. "You can be different from me and I will love you." You don't have to say that out loud—but I'd love to hear it in word as well as action.

Invite me as much as you can—as opposed to demand or command. Most of the wisdoms you've gained and know will come to me through experience—not your expressed observations. Allow me to see the same movie and have a different experience.

Look at me. See me. Ask me who I am often. Once I am confident I am seen, honored, treated with wonder, I will be confident of my place in the world—even if it's evolving—and there'll be no extinguishing of my light. My shine will be fueled by friendly fire. I am, I said, to someone there—you. Me. It is great to be galaxy-buddies, starmates with you. Engage. Make it so.

In the Dark

I was fortunate enough to have had a therapist who saw my family of origin work bubbling up and saw how reticent I was to be "disloyal" to my parents, and how afraid I was to dive into my feelings. She said, "You've convinced me you loved and appreciated your parents." They died in my 30's. "Let's take that love and gratitude for now and put it over here on a shelf. We'll pick it up again later." It was a seminal moment for me. An invitation to explore my emotional truths, all of them. Even, and especially, the dark ones. The ones I would not be proud of. I expressed these in many ways. It was difficult. It was painful. It was truth full. And so, it was freeing. I began to see and accept all of me.

This piece was written well into this process. Over my desk I have a picture of my Dad in uniform (in Germany I believe) playing with a small toy truck in the grass.

Hi Ho

We're all as fragile

    as our upbringing

blind as

    our forebear's

poor as

    our patrimony

'til we start

    working the mine

for

    ourselves

I always liked the "Developer" best. It was the most magic. "Hypo" and the "Fixer" were too tame. I still have a hard time with processes that are merely preparatory or preservative. "Developer" was in the middle pan. When I was a kid, I helped my Dad develop pictures. It would be at night in the kitchen. He couldn't afford a dark room.

A lot of the apparatus for his enlarger was of his own ingenuity and making. I got to stay up late, even on a school night if we got in the middle of something. We always did.

He had been in the Signal Corps, a photographer, in W.W. II. He had also been a mess sergeant and a foot soldier (under Patton) who went through already captured towns to "mop up," as they called it. That was the part that most intrigued me because he was vulnerable in that job. As a photographer, he was the only one doing the shooting. And that's what he brought home. Only *he* did the shooting, and only *he* called the shots.

Like most men of his era, he didn't talk about the really brave (even if idiotic) things of war—like facing possible snipers and stragglers with loaded weapons. I had a sense not to ask him about these things, though they were far and away the stories I wanted most to hear. I wanted him to tell me he was afraid.

By then John Wayne had had his way with the male culture and Dad had had his way with me. Fear was not o.k. In one of the classic backfires of the "I'll-show-you" syndrome, I now have it in spades. Morning noon and night—in my sleep. Yes sir, tell me I can't have it, and I'm tenacious. I release no fear before its time. Perhaps the only one I don't have is that my son will think it's not o.k. to be afraid. I have broken that chain. I have modeled fear. I have reached out for help. I have said I'm not enough, or rather, I don't experience myself as enough, sometimes. That feels good. Strangely good. And I wish he could have shown me that side of himself, my Dad. And he may have, had he lived long enough, and alcohol hadn't done its number on him.

I remember his last day. He was two years into early medical retirement. He had raked some leaves and done some grocery shopping with Mom. She called and said she thought he had had a stroke. I was there before the EMS unit. As they carried him out to the ambulance, his right arm kept falling off the stretcher. I rode in the back right next to him. He was lucid. He could talk. He chose not to, save for one comment on the length of a red light that even a siren didn't get us through. He looked frightened. Scared to death. I

Joe Wise

wished with all my heart he would have said so. His father had had a stroke and was feeble and "helpless" for years. It *had* to be on his mind. He died some few hours later.

If telling someone you are afraid was taboo, then telling another *man* was taboo to the second power and telling your *son* ran off the then known scale. We were a family quite deft at disguising all but the glad feelings—and in their case, we even manufactured some extras.

But those nights in my childhood and youth staying up late to "do" pictures with Dad seem a haven from struggling to do feelings right. Perhaps it was the dark. Perhaps it was the delicious aura of conspiracy. Just we two. In the land of the woman's domain in the day—working as braves and as tradesmen—the squaw and the other papooses off in their sleep.

He'd play with the light with his hands, my Dad, the creator, exposing a face or a hand just a few seconds more to heighten its place in the scene—not just yet, but later in my turf, in the land of the pans. Into the hypo he'd put it and start on the next print, and now it was mine. I'd look at his face in the glow of the red bulb we'd see by, till the light of the enlarger shone through and signaled the start of the next picture's journey. Soon he would nod, and I'd reach with the gigantic tweezers to lift this latest creation out of the hypo and into the developer.

And it would begin to unfold. This one is me. Like a sunrise I start to appear. With the gentle rock and swish of the pan I bring me up, strong—clearer and clearer. I am beautiful. Wearing my Roy Rogers shirt and a black eye. A child of adventure I am. A dreamer and doer. I've been in the battle. Bravely enough to carry a scar. I have a shy but satisfied smile on my face. I would hold it. Into the fixer.

We are quiet in the dark. I stifle a yawn. I wonder who's next.

★　★　★

This piece too is a snapshot in a process. Preceding in this case what we call "forgiveness," but I've known more as "understanding." In the end there really is nothing to forgive each other for—other than being human, and brave enough to live a life, and doing the very best we can with what we have at any given moment.

Click.

Picture of Self as a Child

The jumping-off point for this entry is to let your consciousness "find" a photo/image of you as a child. Digital, print, slide. If it is hard copy, you or a family member, have it. Either from memory, or an in-hand image, you take five minutes or so to describe it. Almost like a reporter. Who's in it? Who are they to you (If you're not alone). How old are you? What are you wearing? How about your hair? Is this inside or outside? Describe the location? Time of year?

Now, take twenty (minutes), and "find out"—who is this child? What is his world like? What does it feel like to be her? What are his hopes and dreams? What are her realities? Likes and dislikes? Wants? Surrenders?

I find different pictures reveal different aspects of me and my early journey. I can even "enter" the same picture later and find out I can't step in the same river twice. The image, although fixed, has its own fluidity. Me and the river dance "alone," till we meet again.

I am standing on the sidewalk in front of my house on 22nd Street just south of Garland in Louisville, Kentucky. I will later learn Cassius Clay (not yet Muhammad Ali) lives five blocks away. I am about 10 years old. I have no shirt on. I am tan. Shorts. Khaki. No shoes. It is summer and not too hot. I am standing in a group. My sister Jul, she's 7. And Chick from around the corner on Date Street. He's blond, handsome and 12 or 13. And Jimmy from across the street. Gangly. Dark greasy hair and about 12 too. I think my Mom took this picture. It is black and white.

★ ★ ★

Who are these people? People I've surrounded myself with? They are the three allies I have in three different worlds. Jul, my family world. Chick, my neighborhood hero. Jimmy, my flirt with the dark side.

Jul, my sister. I was commissioned by Mom and Dad to look out for her. I didn't like that job. It felt too adult, too cramping. But I *did* like her. She was up for fun and didn't make herself demanding or needy to me. Later in life we became further good buddies. We never shared on the dynamics of our family—most kids of alcoholics didn't in those days—but we *did* share new adventures and could keep secrets. I trusted her.

Chick was well built, good looking, a great athlete. I wanted to be all that. I am of a little build, average looking, pretty good athlete. Chick was also courteous and caring with adults. He genuinely looked for ways to serve big and little people. He's wearing a shirt, while Jimmy and I don't. Jul's in a sun suit. Chick is not resisting the summer with his shirt. He just seems more comfortable with it on. It's just as good for me. He has a big chest. I would look even smaller.

Jimmy is a little shifty and morose and plotting. He likes what all the adults call "trouble." He skips school. I wouldn't dare. He doesn't have a dad like mine. He doesn't have a dad. His mom works, and I don't think she can stay up with Jimmy. Not many could. He sneaks around. With him I play with matches. Wouldn't dare at home.

This pattern sets up for my life. I cultivate three sets of friends. Family, world-light, and world-dark. This world family (light, dark) shows up big time in the same person for me a few months later. In Donny. He is 14, I think. In the 8th grade for the second time. Is way big for his age. Good looking. Brash talker. Slicked back hair. Leather jacket in winter. White T-shirt with Camels rolled in the sleeve in summer.

Donny teaches me how to serve Mass. The guys tell me he heads a gang. A rough gang. Just out of our neighborhood. He's been arrested a couple of times. I don't know what for. I don't think I want to know. He looks like somebody who really is as tough as he looks. I had already experienced the devastation of power in an older male with my Dad. Here's somebody, almost my age, who I think could take him. I am secretly pleased that such an event could be a possibility. It gives me hope. The game taught to me feels mostly like dominance and submission. Somebody dominates, wins, rules. The other serves. It would be later in my life before I fully opened to cooperation as a possible scheme for living.

Donny is great with me. He doesn't get upset when I don't get the Latin right away. He rehearses me patiently. I am shocked. He looks so different at a distance. He sees I can't lift the heavy Mass book on the stand to move it for the gospel, so he says, "I'll make sure you get somebody strong to serve with you, till you get bigger." No ridicule. No impossible expectations. All the Dad expectations. I wanted to tell all the bad-mouthers of Donny to shut up. I didn't have the courage. Whatever else he was doing with his life, I felt I wanted to try, so I could be as patient and as gentle as he was with me.

He was the first male I knew to offer me an alternative. I "dated" his sister Mary Francis for a while when I was 13. I hoped I'd learn more about Donny. I did. He was in juvenile prison. Later it would be "big people" prison. The year I left for the Seminary, Mary Francis got pregnant. 15 years old. I knew it wasn't me. I liked her, too.

Wholly, Holy, Wholly

I had to give up my white bucks. It was 1953 and I was 13. I had signed up to go to the seminary. It was like a boarding school for Catholic priests, or rather for boys who wanted to be priests. I was going to approach it like extended Boy Scouts. You even had to wear a uniform. Dark blue suits on Sundays; and dark pants, white shirts and solid color dark ties for school; and black shoes all the time. So the white bucks had to go and so did my really cool powder blue and white striped seersucker pants.

Pat Boone was making the bucks popular. I liked Pat Boone, then. I liked to imitate his voice. I crooned good. I could even whistle the bridge to "Love Letters in the Sand." Pat Boone made it ok for a mild mannered white guy to do "Tutti Fruiti."

Why had I decided to go to the seminary? I could never date or get married, and I had just mastered the art of the five-minute kiss in Barbara's coal bin. The feelings in my lips were really something, but the part I remember most was mingling my breath with hers. She had the sweetest breath. No more of that.

I think two big reasons were Father Knopp and Father Vessels. One took me fishing, the other took me to funerals. Father Knopp was the fisher man and showed me how to bait a hook and cast, and teased me when I'd jump away from a blue gill flipping on the line. Just when I'd get the nerve to wrap my hand around him and de-hook him, he'd flip and flop and Father Knopp would laugh. Father Vessels was the funeral man. I was a server at the altar, and every time there was a funeral, Father Vessels had to pick five servers, and we would all get up in the middle of the class, most of us not even *trying* to hide our glee, and go over to church and start begging him to let us be one of the two, who would get to go to the cemetery after the Funeral Mass. If you got to go to the cemetery, you'd have to be gone till after lunch, and that meant he would treat you to a hamburger and a milk shake. He often wrestled with a lot of us on the front lawn, in front of the priests' house. His boss, the pastor, didn't like that. We did.

Now here comes the boss of the seminary, Father White, to my house on Date Street, to talk to me, and Mom and Dad about me being a priest. Right in the middle, Mom jumps up and goes and gets a picture I drew, and she framed, of a crucifix with no Jesus on it—just a draped cloth over both arms of the sideways board, standing tall over the city of Jerusalem. Father White looks at it and I wish she hadn't shown him. I didn't get the folds in the cloth on the left hand side to hang real natural. I wanted him to just guess I could do it better. Father White says there's a Jim from my parish that was in the opening year of the seminary (mine was to be the second year of the school's existence) and that he was a straight A student. My Dad says, "Now that gives you something to shoot for." I vow I will to myself. Six years later I gunned him down with a Suma Cum Laude.

I begin to get a sense that *everybody* thinks this is something special. That *I* am something special. My friends' parents start treating me differently. I am the only one in my class going to be a priest. It is like I am already a little bit of a priest before I even go. I love the feeling. I begin to see myself saying Mass, and all the people watching me and being thankful I'm the star in the most important thing they do.

In the last week before September, I begin to notice Billy and Larry and C.J. and I don't meet to play the pin ball machine at Cooksie's Grill before our scout meeting. I'm not meeting at Victory Park for pick up football with them either. They are going to a regular high school. I don't know how to say goodbye.

I try to think of seminary as Boy Scouts again. The longest I have been away from home is Boy Scout Summer Camp, for one week, at Covered Bridge. I focus on the fun I had then—rough-housing with the assistant scout master, sneaking into the woods at night and skinny dipping by moonlight, putting a frog in Larry's sleeping bag. I try to think seminary is all this plus, I get to know God very closely.

The day of entry jumps into my life like a Mickey Mantle line drive, even though it's all I ever thought of for weeks. I have received my checklist from the seminary. What to bring. What to not. What to wear. What to not. I leave my white bucks to my brother. He is four sizes too small for them. When I leave I lose track of them.

Standing in line with thirty nine other tender reeds and ancient suitcases, I wait to check in with "the Rector." This is Father White's new name. I will come to know him as a man of many "by goshes" and "by gollys," of radiant twinkles of the eye, welcoming embraces, an easy hugger, a hearty laugher, a disciplined leader with a flair for the dramatic. I will find out he was once called on to exorcise, or chase the devil out of, a building on the big Island of Hawaii. He was tall, angular of frame, with a sharp flint-struck face, capped by a shock of white hair. He would stride down the corridors with a bounce and a limp (perhaps where the devil nicked him). Since he was the rector, he couldn't be my confessor.

My checklist had told me I would need a confessor. He would be a faculty member I would go to confession to all the time and would be my main guide, my new father. Just then Father MacMurray walks up to me in line. He has been greeting all the other freshmen. He looks nervous. He shakes all the time. I would learn the students call him "Black Mac." He wears a large black cape over his black-buttoned cassock. His black, greased-back hair sits on top a round, squat, reddish face. He's always chewing a cigar. He breathes in snorts. I would come to know him as volatile, a lot like my Dad. Every time he lit a cigar or a pipe, there was so much energy in the air around him, I thought he might blow up. He became my confessor for the next six years. "Hello," he says, "my name is Father MacMurray." He extends a shaking palm. I shake it, and he re-lights his cigar. I don't know what to say.

By 8:30 they have shown us all the huge unpopulated rooms with strange names. Refectory. Dormitory. Lavatory. Chapel. Two hours after silence was imposed and lights were out in this twenty-bed room, I am still wide awake. I think of my new dark clothes. They are all in a metal locker in the next room. At home they were always in the same room with me—in a wooden chest of drawers. They told us we would awaken in silence and not speak till after morning prayers and Mass. I see my bathrobe on a metal chair beside my bed. I've never owned a bathrobe. It seems too formal. Too grown up. There are no curtains on the windows, no rugs on the marble floors, no lamps. I am too young and afraid to know I miss these. I am too unnurtured in my alcoholic home to know I miss comfort and a safe emotional place.

I know as my pen hits this paper, I did not want to be in the seminary and I did not want to go back home. My "survival" instincts and skills would keep me in the safer of the two for ten and one half years.

And though I still struggle today with giving myself permission to fully enjoy many of the pleasures of this world, I have resolutely chosen
> to keep my clothes in the same room
> to seek out peaceful guides
> to draw with less concern about the naturalness of the folds
> to not shoot for anybody or anything
> to ditch my bathrobe
> to mingle my breath with a lover
> to wrestle with my son
> to treat my daughter as I would the tenderest part of my soul.

Welcome back, Joe.

Joe Wise

At 13

I put the numbers 12 through 21 on little pieces of folded paper into a bowl and draw out two. The two are to give me some choice in a "random" experience. Like life. The number is my age. I explore who I am at 13. My choice today. It helps me to "be there" again by writing in the present tense. I didn't "slow down" enough to fully notice much of this at the time. It's why I find the teen years so rich with "path" information and pieces to re-claim.

Like a significant photo, I can re-visit for new discoveries.

I am 13. I am starting to grow again. I was in the first row of two in my graduation class. 5'2" is way below what I wanted. Dad is 6'. I want to be 6'4". I want to weigh more than him. I want to be big enough not to be scared of him. I don't think there's any other way not to be. I have tried everything else. I do brave, maybe really crazy, things sometimes. I try to be great at everything. I was the only guy in my class who was a jock *and* a brain. I am signed up for the Roman Catholic Seminary. This is a weird summer. Larry and C.J. have stopped asking me to do stuff with them. Maybe they think I'm too holy now. I can't ask them. That's not in my training—silent training—not-really-knowing-it-was-training training. I have so many things I can't say—and don't say. It would be too disloyal. I hold to myself my Dad's drinking and rage. My Mom's drinking and shrinking. I don't want to be rageful or shrinking. I don't talk about this to myself, much less to my brothers and sisters—not to the priests, not to the nuns. Most of my Aunts and Uncles drink a lot too.

I'm banking on priests, especially the ones who run the seminary, not being mad or shrinking. The seminary is a nice out for me. I can leave home at 13 and be thought brave, cool, holy even. I need to be admired. (Nobody told me about this need). Some people have already started to treat me a little bit like a priest. I love it. It's one of the many extras, as I give myself to knowing God and helping people.

I wish I knew how to say goodbye to my friends.

I don't know anybody going to, or already in, the seminary.

It will be a haven. Priests don't hit children or spank them or use a belt on them. That's a huge plus. They don't have to go to war. They do seem a little out-of-it. But I'll be different. I won't be out-of-it. I'll show everybody that God can be in the world and love it. He can love Chuck Berry and Elvis and Fats Domino. He can love basketball and hiking and picnics. Real picnics—not the ones they have where you have to bet money on cake wheels.

It really takes a load off deciding what to do with my life. I've got 12 years mapped out in getting prepared, and the bishop takes care of me from then on. I'll always have a house, and peanut butter, a car, and toothpaste. It comes with the job.

I'm relieved I won't have to date girls. I've had great times with Judy and Mary Francis—but I don't like the possibility of getting rejected. I like to be the one to say goodbye. Like when I told *them* I was going to be a priest. I love the feelings I had with them. I love kissing—exchanging a sweetness of breath with Barbara. No more. I need to get myself set for this Fall. September in the seminary. Out of my home. I am clever to figure this out. I can count on me to take care of myself. Go Joe.

Singing in Talent Show at St. Mary's

I am 20 years old. I have been given a chance to sing in the talent show here in the seminary in Baltimore. I am 800 miles from home. I have been living most of the year (9 months) since I was 12, away from my family. We don't leave the grounds for entertainment. It is forbidden. We can't watch movies here or listen to the radio. Once a year we have these talent shows. I've never been in one.

They feel too much like showing off for me to get in one. But I'm going to. I feel a strange conflict inside. I want to sing. I don't want to sing. Singing is a full expression of myself. I like that. I might forget the words or miss the notes. I may miss when to come in with the piano. The guys may say to themselves and not to me, "What the heck is he thinking? Does he think he's good?" I also might be really good, and better than most, and I'll go beyond them, and they'll be mad at me for having the gift, because they didn't get it.

"The Rose of Tralee." I am Irish. But it's a *new* song to me. Will the priests look at me funny or judge me because it's a love song? I've tried to shut that part of myself down and off. I won't be getting married. Not and be a priest. Lousy tradeoff—but that's the way it is.

The pressure of doing this dead right and perfect is mounting. They're even gonna put me in costume and make up. Lights. Microphones. Almost 200 guys and about 2 dozen faculty members. What an audience. I hope I don't forget the words.

I did fine. It wasn't perfect. The guys went nuts. I have a good voice. I put my heart into the song. It wasn't mechanical. I discovered the fear goes away after I start. By the second verse I was into only the song, and not me singing the song. I love this feeling. Doing this. *And* the response. Will I have to wait till next year to do it again? I've got to come up with some other times and places.

Two years later I picked up a guitar and began to write, compose, and sing. I find many places and times to sing, and to bring what I've written to the outside, and trust it to strangers. My innate shyness has not stopped me. This is amazing. Unlike anything I could have thought up or planned ahead of time.

I go on to having this being my ticket of entry into expressing my views, and speaking to large gatherings. It earns me enough money to care for my household, and raise two children.

It is a gift of great grace.

Picking up Guitar

There is a nameless completeness I have always found and felt in music. Like words, a pointer to the Truth of Being. Having the gift and joy, oftentimes ecstasy of listening to or performing it, having it course through me is grace of the highest order.

And music took shape in me from the matrix of my personal history (family, seminary) and my communal history (the 60's).

Like my teens, I was so busy "doing" my life, I didn't stop in my twenties to consciously look at all of my accompanying feelings and motivations, including the not so lofty. Some of these entries in my journal do.

I am 22. I am in the Catholic Seminary. 800 miles from home. Thank God. In Baltimore. St. Mary's. My choirmate, Charley, has a guitar. A Sears Silvertone. I am amazed the faculty lets him have it. It is so worldly. He plays it only in the rec room—not his room. Rules. He obeys that one. All of 'em as far as I can see. During Christmas break, I heard a record by Joan Baez. The sweetest voice. Velvet feminine, singing songs that bite, rip, call for change, outrage. The plane wreck over Los Gatos Canyon—a plane full of migrant workers. Buried nameless. Woody Guthrie gave her the tune and lyric: *"All they will call them is just deportees."* She was championing these people. And love songs about breaking away from parents. Her mom sleeping with a silver dagger, to kill her daughter's lover, who she really *really* doesn't like. Blindly doesn't like. Prejudice.

Not knowing him. And I heard Pete Seeger singing "We Shall Overcome." A simple guitar. An everyday voice—championing a race other than his own. This was all so electric. And the guitar wasn't Chuck Berry or Duane Eddy or Les Paul or Bill Haley, all my favorites. It wasn't electric. But it was. *Acoustic* I learned it was called.

Just like Charley's. I ask him if I can try it. He says sure. The strings are harder to push down than I thought. They are steel. They cut the ends of my fingers. Charley says, "Don't worry, my blood is on there too." In an age of Aids, which this wasn't, maybe a transfer point for disease. Neither of us were sexually active or dopers—so I guess I would have been alright. The drive to play, may even have pushed me through this risk.

I now see I saw this instrument as a weapon of choice. Music the ammunition. Target: (passive aggressively) the establishment. My Mom and Dad and their think-alike peers. The government. The Church. All the areas of duplicity in these. The powers that be defining me, telling me what is right, wrong, availing unto salvation. Especially all the parts that trampled (though not on purpose maybe) individuality, self-possession, uniqueness, disagreement. Target: people who ignore oppression, enslave, in subtle, and not so subtle ways, other humans. I will have a voice.

Even in my home. My Dad loves the Ames Brothers and Perry Como—Mom too—I'll get my voice sounding like theirs and sing the songs of freedom. A spoonful of sugar to help the medicine go down. I'll be listened to at home, by the Church, that belittles people who are not priests (it'll be my insurance in case I don't become a priest), by the politicians, by the mayor, and city council wrestling with open housing.

This is quite a weapon, quite a tool. I can't believe I didn't take the chance to start playing when I was 10, and Mom and Dad asked me if I wanted to. They would have bought me lessons. I was too big into sports. I'm glad about that. I wouldn't surrender or trade those.

But this is cool now. With 3 to 6 positions on the frets, and a capo to change keys, I can play almost any folk song ever written. The words are easy for me to memorize.

My Dad buys me a Gibson C-1 classic. The action is 1000% smoother and easier than Charley's. The sound is rich, full. My voice is too.

I'm off to a 23-year career, that takes me around the world. A little guy with a big voice. Later, a bigger guy with a big voice. What a gift.

Music and Me

In the early 60's (my early 20's) I fell in love with Vanguard and Folkways records. Actually with who I found there. Joan Baez, Pete Seeger, Leadbelly, Doc Watson, Leon Bibb, Ian and Sylvia, Odetta. The "pop" market was giving me Bob Dylan, Peter Paul and Mary, the Weavers, Gordon Lightfoot, Tom Paxton, Judy Collins. I was giving myself guitar lessons. Few things hurt as much as my left hand after a time-forgetting session on my borrowed Sears Silvertone guitar. In the beginning I came to expect blood. Few things felt as good as mastering an "F" chord and letting "Staid on Freedom" (Odetta's version) flow through me. With or without others to hear or join.

My parents had mercy on my student budget and bought me a Gibson C-I classical guitar. Pure gold to me. *And* my fingers. I set right out to learn Red Rosey Bush, Leon Bibb's version, and felt immediately the vastness of terrain opening up to me, for me, and eventually for others through me.

I was in the R. C. Seminary during these days. The Roman Church was haltingly leaning into Pope John XXIII's *aggiornamento* (roughly "catching up" with the world) invitation. The average Catholic's main connection with their Church was the Mass, and that was on the "updating" docket. For us in America it meant primarily English instead of Latin. All of us, I believe, immediately felt a loss of elements that seemed to foster the mystical. One big one was Latin. I had memorized much of the Latin used in liturgy by age ten, allowing me to be an "altar boy." By my early twenties, I had 6 years studying the ins and outs of the language and about 4 years of taking some of my classes, texts, and lectures, in Latin. I've always loved words and the sound of them, so this was no "task" for me. Still, at this juncture, to let go of a "dead" language in an evolving world seemed like a great thing to 22-year-old me. We could and would find our mystical prompts and moments and vehicles elsewhere, even in the "new" liturgies. Ultimately nature and silence, always available to all, easily re-ascended for me as the holy of holies.

Meanwhile, here is a dead certain hierarchic church, running for years an interpretation of the Last Supper as liturgy, in rituals that "belonged" more and more to the ordained—the male ordained—changing its course in favor of the people of the pews. Pews. Things not needed at the circular supper. Quiet. A thing we could have easily and often in the old *and* new.

For me, though, having a voice, having everybody have a voice was the richest vein, the biggest artery to and through the heart. Sung word only amplified this. We knew this already from our Gregorian Chant. Now, it would be in *our* words, English, and from *our* world, contemporary. We began with not-so-contemporary but available. Songs, hymns mostly, by earlier English-speaking or translated theologians and catechists. Wesley, Luther. "Praise God from who all blessings flow"—wherever He might be. "To Thee above the skies"—oh, that's where He is. I could not pray these. I set out to write some *for me*. With more direct communication, more personal, more intimate. "Gonna sing my Lord… for all that I'm worth… till I see your face." Looking back, this, one of my first songs, was my outward voicing of the desire for awakened awareness, enlightenment—my *om*.

"Take Our Bread" was my actual first song to write as prayer at *public* liturgy. In the early 70's, while attending a Mass in Rome, I was astonished to find it in the parish's customized song sheets. Eventually it found a home in the International Methodist Hymnal. With Wesley. And Luther. It began its journey as a hard sell. Not to the people who sang it with me and asked for the chords and words so they could pray it elsewhere. Just to the eventual publisher.

Maleita and I, our wedding just ahead of us, were traveling to Ohio with my cousin Maggie to the Glenmary Sisters' annual fair and fund raiser. On the way we stopped at World Library of Sacred Music in Cincinnati. Father Clarence Rivers was published by them. I loved his music and was singing it long before I met him. That first meet with Clarence took place around a campfire. I sang some of my songs. At the end of the night he said I should record them. I said, "I don't have the money." He said, "Now you do." He sent me that money with one proviso: that *I* produce the recording. No publisher he was aware of would know how. It was a different animal in "sacred music" circles. He said if the recording didn't sell, he wanted nothing back. If it did, he only wanted back what he gave me. It was such a pleasure to return that money, that energy to him. I am confident it was recycled in another pay-it-forward bequest we've all unwittingly benefited from.

There were other gifts from Clarence over the years. The sight of the child in him emerging so easily and often with Michelle, our young one. And this one. In the immediate aftermath of Martin Luther King's assassination, he called me and asked me if I would do the music at some Masses with him in the Watts area of L. A. I said yes before I let myself feel how scary this might be. I told him of a new killer twelve-string Fender a friend had given me. And added I probably wouldn't be taking it with me, since it was so expensive and I thought it would be flashy in such a poor neighborhood. There was a long pause. "Joseph. I will be wearing my very finest vestments. When else could they experience them?" I packed my 12-string.

World Library was new to me. Any music house was new to me. I already felt confident asking them to publish the sheet music to my first collection of songs because they had published Clarence. It wasn't the slam dunk I had envisioned. Granted, the three of us, Maggie, Maleita and I were dressed in cutoff jeans and tee shirts, ready to work at the Glenmary Fair. I asked at the front desk to see the owner, Mr. Omer Westendorff.

He came out and took us into his office. I told him I had some songs, would he like to publish them. He said, "Where are your manuscripts?" I said, "I don't read music." There was more than a moment for him to take that in. Then he said, "Do you have a little recording of them?" I said, "Not yet, but I am going to record them in a studio." And I had word sheets I could give him, and I had my guitar in the car, and we could sing them live for him. There was again a long, and I hoped pregnant, pause before he said, "I'll call my staff together." Everybody jammed into his office. The three of us sat on the floor and sang to them. We sang "Take Our Bread." When we finished it, there was complete silence. Omer picked up his word sheet and said, "Yours, as we eat the bread our hearts can't forget." Pause. "Now, does our heart have a memory?" My heart fell. I looked up at the drawings of his nephews and nieces he had pinned up all around. Had I misread him? I said out loud, "Mine does."

We sang a couple more songs. The staff said nothing. Omer would once in a while ask questions or make an observation. He had heretofore published pretty much nothing but hymns for the people in the pews. "So this is, I guess, folk music and it's ok to repeat things, huh?"

At the end of the session he floored me by saying he'd "take them." We signed a contract. He paid me a dollar. The going legal rate. With royalties on sales down the road.

A year went by. It included recording my *Gonna Sing My Lord* album, my first, two weeks before we got married; our wedding; my beginning travels to sing these songs; and Michelle's birth. In 1966 all that was available to me was to record monaurally. We sang the songs, all instruments and voices into the booth. The engineer recorded it. At the end of the session he pulled the tape spool off the deck and we walked out with it. No mixing. No discreet channels. Just as well. I was mostly interested in how the recording *felt*. The technical parts were only to serve *that*. That was the first of 21 albums in 22 years I wrote and produced. At the end of the first year of *Gonna Sing My Lord*'s release, I went back to Omer and said, "How's the sheet music coming?" Many were asking for it. He said it was taking a long time to get the *nihil obstat* and *imprimatur* for it. I was dumbfounded at this. Basically a bishop having to ok it. That was the last collection where that was an issue or requirement. Was never either for me. It was also the beginning of a real softening by Omer, toward me and, I think, overall. He got married. I think for the first time. In his 60's I believe. Had a child. Which he delivered, though, of course, not by design. Great, brave changes in my eyes.

I went on to other publishers as "my kind" of music became more prevalent. Before he died Omer told me he often found himself singing my songs to himself in the mirror as he shaved. It was the wedding I had always intended: the sacred and the secular, the everyday and the transcendent, the Soul and the Spirit.

I felt like a nephew being pinned up and honored on his wall. *And* grateful for the chance to be of some service throughout the world "library," to many hearts and souls.

Meeting Maleita

He met her at Fontaine House. Her name was Maleita. If he could find her, he was going to ask her to be the third member of our team to give an upcoming high school senior retreat. Our second one. John had been a priest for fourteen years before someone asked him to venture in this direction. He called me. "I can't bear to give these young people the kind of retreat I had when I was a senior. Would you come on board?" It is the early 60's. This would be new for me too. Yes. We decided we wouldn't call it anything, especially "a retreat"—but might let the seniors name it at the end of the weekend. The major part of our planning was not to plan. Friday night was just about all we prepared for, including a free-for-all session we hoped would give us all direction running toward Sunday evening. And run we did, winging it most of the way. It was a life changing experience for many of us. A wonderful mix of hilarity and grace, tears and fears, trust and pride, standing tall and out loud, sitting in peace. "Community Wing Ding" got the most votes for a title. I liked it because it included the biggest elements for me: a non-hierarchical gathering, with input from all; the winging or seat-of-the-pantsness of the whole phenomenon; and the "ding" of the bell of true-to-lifeness and clear authenticity.

We were gearing up for "C.W.D. Two." Or whatever this new gathering would name itself. John's improbable task of finding Maleita (no last name) in a city of almost a million people seemed a bust from the beginning. But he really wanted her. The book discussion he met her at, held at Fontaine House (I had never heard of it) explored *The*

Art of Loving, by Eric Fromm. He loved her comments and insights, met her briefly as she held a cookie tray at break time, and if he could only remember the parish she said she belonged to... and suddenly he did. He called the pastor of a huge parish at way the other end of town and said, "Do you have or know a Maleita?" He did. John called her. Nobody was asking lay people (as we were called then) to give retreats. She, after some thought, said yes. John said "I think you'll like her." This became for me the understatement of the century. At our 25th wedding anniversary, John, now married with children, read the entry from his journal the day he introduced us. I was keeping a journal only with my heart then. It began to fill up fast. At one of our first meetings—sitting on a basement floor, we were talking about whether there was Divine Presence in all sentient beings— and she said: "I could, and do, love a rock, whatever is in it." Though I don't remember it consciously, something deep and true in me sat straight up and smiled. My focus (looking back) with the Church I was raised in, was to see if it would tolerate more inclusiveness at every level, about almost everything. Doesn't a flower have as much spiritual authority as a Pope? Who are we to exclude any form or individual from the Divine Expression, the Formless's Extravagance? At the moment, I was distracted from all this, even as I was noticing how companioned I felt; and how attracted I was to this almost-never-found woman.

The retreat weekend was a return to bliss for me. Feeling fully authentic, engaged, of service. We are still in touch, even visiting-wise with some souls who were "on" that weekend.

Meanwhile I am signed up for a September to September Masters program in D. C. She, for studies at the University of Louisville. It was not easy. The separation. We did the best we could to remedy that with a letter a day. For a year. Ten months in, I find on the outside of a Friday letter to me in a strange hand I later discover is that of her mailman, the words: Get her a ring. He came to our wedding. Felt he was an integral part of our courtship. Shot movies. Brought an extravagant gift. But these months apart allowed me only to give her a ring over the wires. Sunday nights. All I could

Joe Wise

save during the week went into the pay phone on the corner, so we could talk. I was washing dishes for room and board. Once in a while, some friends would let me call her from the warmth of their apartments.

I was caught up in the most wonderful confluence of my life. I was deeply in love with her *and* with what I was doing. What I was doing, I/we were making up as we went along. Turning down desk jobs, I stayed open to something wider. I was composing, writing, singing, giving retreats. The Universe came to meet us. The gift of a house for our first year, Fontaine House, as Vernon, an Episcopal priest who owned it, went to Rome to become a Catholic Priest. A dry wit, he sent us a closeup picture of his re-ordination by the Pope, just the two of them, with the caption: I'm on the left.

Fontaine House was a community house downstairs—open for scheduled meetings. The very house John met Maleita in. The house we were living in when I produced and recorded my first album. It was named after the Fontaine family, who in early Louisville history operated a ferry across the Ohio not far from here. It seemed a good name for our recording label, crossing over and connecting everyday life with the transcendent—moving back and forth till we knew them as one.

Another priest, Ben, who with John was running the Catholic parish that looked most like the community we had found in our retreat work, with the addition of in-the-neighborhood social outreach —Ben, had asked me what it would take to keep us afloat while we turned down desk jobs elsewhere in the country. Whatever that is, he said, he would pay us, to stay in Louisville and work with his people on improving Sunday services. Until, he said, the national invitations I was starting to receive for concerts and talks and retreats could carry us. That point came within the year. It was a crucial gift for the trajectory my/our life took.

We became increasingly conscious of how much these things were not "givens" even as they were given. This awareness grows the further away I come from this period and the immense, beautiful, grinding, exhilarating, exhausting sublime experience it was. And all of it completely unimaginable and maybe even undoable, certainly not in the exact form it unfolded, without *this* companion—the cookie server with a great take on the art of loving.

And rocks.

Of Screwdrivers and Marshmallows

Well, the cage we had built to keep the raccoons from strewing our garbage all over the driveway was losing a door. The cage was for the garbage cans, not the raccoons. The little devils had pried, torn, chewed or weaseled their way into every can we had ever bought, and through every device we'd ever devised, to secure it. In a last-ditch effort we called a carpenter and said build us a fortress. (Build it and they will come).

What he delivered with his helpers was formidable—a massively framed horizontal cage you could just as easily see a lion pacing in as being the quiet home of three stalwart Sears finest refuse containers. (Come see the harder side of Sears). It has proven to be a decisive maneuver in a long and crafty battle.

We had started with a simple twenty-gallon metal can with a snug fitting lid. No contest. The little bandits robbed us blind—weeks of pilfering and messing up the driveway while we persisted in disbelief. Bandits. That's what they are. Breaking and entering is their game. They even come with those little built-in masks.

We stepped things up by bringing on our tanks—thirty-gallon duratough hard plastic models with built-in metal clamps to secure the lid. A joke. More weeks of disbelief. Followed by our twine gambit. Seal the can with clamps, then run a line of twine between the clamps over the lid. Tie the whole package with a mesmerizing series of square knots, loop knots, timber knots, anchor knots and my own signature—the dread knot. Morning found the driveway looking like a rerun, with the entire length of twine laying neatly, knotless, on the lawn. Raccoons—29. Wises—Zip.

Bailing wire was next. Elaborate wrappings and bindings culminating in a spiral twist I could manage only with a pair of needlenose pliers and sealed by screwing on one of those plastic covers you use for electrical wire couplings. Child's play.

All this is happening, mind you, while we feed the little Houdinis every night on our back deck. I love 'em on our back deck. They're a pain in the can out on the driveway. We feed them marshmallows. I continue with the blind belief that this will somehow diminish their desire for plebeian food, secondhand fare, garbage. Nope.

Once, my daughter studied their habits for several weeks as part of a science project. Early on, a fat momma came up deckside to eat. A couple of weeks later, she reappears with her new babies in tow. The kids make moves on the marshmallows, and the mother swats them away. We are all dismayed at this cruel and heartless approach to motherhood. Over the next several nights, the pattern continues. Then one night, the little coon kids turned it around. They started battling the momma for their share of the *booty*. After some extended tussling, they *all* ended up hunched on their back legs, holding their marshmallows deftly in their front paws and chewing away. I could swear the momma was smiling. My daughter says, "Yeah! Teenage raccoons!"

I suspect mom and dad also train the little varmints to burgle. No, more than burgle. To do battle. Reconnoiter. Strategize. Move in for the kill. They're turning out a pack of rummaging Rommels, the Garbage Foxes. And until I ordered the fortress, I was no match for them.

It came, the cage, with stout four-by-four framing and heavy metal webbing. It took three strapping men to load it down. It also came with a hasp on the front door for a lock. In one final act of respect for the opposition, I opted for the *key* lock over the *combination* one.

And we have since lived an impregnable existence, garbage-wise, while our marshmallow parties take place with lighthearted banter and no hidden grudges. I suspect there are a couple of neighbors close by who are just entering the initial stages of Garbage Wars.

Now, early this Saturday, I begin assembling the tools I'll need to fix the door. Actually, the *hinges* on the door. My partner, my son John, has agreed to forego an extra hour of sleep to lend me a hand. Later, we are going out to Freedom Hall to see if we can find somebody with extra tickets to the University of Louisville-Memphis State game. Pre-season tickets are sewed up. Extras, on site, right before gametime always seem to materialize.

We have done this ritual before, John and I-the ticket search not the hinge change. I have done very little handyman stuff in my career as a homeowner. Partly because I was thoroughly engrossed in my bread-earning jobs, partly because I could afford to hire someone to do repairs, and partly because I had had such a rough experience helping *my* Dad do these things when I was a kid. Conditioning runs deep. I still feel twinges of shame about not being able to do electrical and plumbing stuff. Then my sanity returns, and I tell myself: You chose to learn how to write and play guitar. That's ok. Then my competitive self clicks in and says: Yeah, and there aren't too many homeowners out there that know an F-sharp-diminished-flat-five-chord either. Neither do I, but I know a lot of others.

My Saturdays as a kid helping Dad were pretty painful. I was a bright, inquisitive, resourceful little guy, and none of that was fostered during the long and tedious hours of Saturdays. I held boards, handed nails, ran for tools, brought his beers, and cleaned up. What I really wanted to do was use the hammer and screw-drivers. Or have him talk to me. Or both. My one or two forays with tools was greeted with "here, give me that, you dummy."

Dad seemed always too concentrated on what he was doing to talk to me or show me how to use the tools. Patience was not something I experienced in my Dad. He seemed to give it all to the people on his floor at the American Tobacco Co. He was a fore-man. Only now do I know that I hated all those people for robbing me of so much tolerance and understanding and tenderness. For wrecking my suppers. For living in dread of a lump in my Dad's mashed potatoes. For all the silent meals. I hated those people and all the perfect cigarettes they made. And I hated whoever got my Dad started going this way, his father probably, and how secret we all kept this dynamism.

Today I am partnering with John. I take out a screw. He takes out a screw. I drill a hole. He drills a hole. I mount a hinge. He mounts the other. It is a process not without stress. It goes against all my training. We take turns running for needed items. He strips a screw. I do not feel patient. But I do patient things. We are significantly inefficient time wise and work wise. We are remarkable in our cooperation.

I look forward to the game. I don't particularly enjoy ticket hunting among scalpers and the uncertainty about actually getting in, but its a vulnerability and an equal-footing-kind-of-thing I would have loved to have had with *my* Dad. John and I seem to have a fairly equal quotient of fanaticism about Cardinal basketball.

One of my fondest dreams was realized a few winters ago when we got chosen in on different teams in a pickup game over at the local center. We guarded each other. We were both tentative with each other for a few trips up and down the court. Then we both held our own. Passages.

John would be moving out soon. Many who had fostered him along in his journey, highlighted by a struggle with a learning disability, gave us little hope this might happen. Nobody told John. He told *us* of his plan about three months ahead of time so *we*, he said, could have time to get used to it. I still remember the first time he visited us and around ten o'clock startled me with: "Well Mom and Dad, I have to be heading *home*." Not "to my apartment." "Home."

Some few months later I am coming "home" from Circuit City with John. He has asked me to help him pick out a stereo for his new space. I feel honored. This is as close as I can come, I guess, to feeling like a chieftain caught up in a mentoring rite with his brave. We arrive at his apartment home, and he says he would like to prepare a meal for me. He asks me to sit down and relax, and presently I am served the most wonderful bowl of Campbell's Chunky Vegetable Soup, garnished with my favorite accompaniment—Wheatsworth Crackers. John does not like Wheatsworth Crackers.

Lunch is cleared, and we move to the center of the living room area of his studio apartment, where John begins to uncrate the many parts that will make up the stands and cabineting, to hold and house the components of his new sound system. He hands me a couple of screwdrivers and some pliers. "Do you want me to use these?" I say, sitting by the heap.

"No," he says, "I would like you to hold them for me, and hand them to me when I need them, and read the directions out loud to me." I became profoundly aware that it is Saturday, and I am holding tools. I cannot think of anything in the known universe that would hold near this significance and benediction for me.

John is kneeling in the pile of panels, braces, brackets, shelves, and screws, beginning to sort them out as I read. He is a half beat ahead of me in intuition. The assemblage begins. And I see him as a five-year-old struggling to find sounds that would mean the same to us as they did to him. I see him as a young warrior, day after day, in his special schools doing battle with the confusion in his head, while staying clear in his heart. I see him as an eight-year-old "college student" in a residency program at Indiana University, thrown into a last ditch effort to expand his language skills—enough, we hope, to give him a wider berth in this world. I wonder about all the times he followed us, when we might well have followed him. I remember the mornings he drank Pepto Bismol for breakfast, during a stretch of merciless cruelty by some of his classmates at a vo-tech school. I see him as a beaming high school graduate in procession at the Louisville Gardens, formerly named, the Armory. The Armory. He *has* done battle. Two years later he brightens the Southern Baptist Seminary Chapel, as a graduate of Sullivan Junior College, with a certificate in travel and tourism. I see him as a professional guitarist, a sound engineer, a choral singer, a set builder, a tenacious friend, and now a homemaker. One by one, I've watched him untie the knots, throw off the clamps, break the bonds, decipher the locks, fiercely refuse to be caged in or kept out.

The last of the cabineting is going in place. I don't know how it has all happened. Mercifully, I don't know how *all* this has happened. The big stuff has never been up to me, though my fear often reaches for the reins. I am reminded that I need only show up. Everything in this outer picture will change. My relationship with tools, Saturdays, and men making things, is happily no exception.

Joe Wise

Michelle's Birth

This piece, almost more than any other in this collection, reminds me of the relative poverty of words, and that they can only be pointers. To the event, the reality, the persons, the all-sense experiences, they seek to portray.

She will be married September 22nd. A new beginning. A public new beginning, with her own friends, her own circle, one she has beautifully drawn to herself, created herself.

I remember that small circle she began in—Maleita, me, her and Dr. Denton. I remember how privileged and honored I felt to be there, 33 years ago, when few men were allowed into that circle.

I remember her cresting—like a moon, like a sun, coming forth into our world—vibrant, shaking, crying, quickly onto Mom's body, into Dad's arms, a living sentient life-form, separate from my own—yet part of me. To take part in that whole process—from the joy of sex at the front end, and the thrill of being there at the delivery end—clearly pure gift. I felt powerful—but not over anything. I felt suffused with meaning and purpose—I would get to care for this life—till she could—get to carry her, bounce her, let her explore my face, with her fingers, and her heart, till she knew me, and knew she had made a great choice for a fostering being. One who would be committed to her well-being and support—physical, emotional, spiritual. I knew *I* would be open to what *she* would teach also. It would be Grace. Interchange.

I felt I stood with co-creators and fathers everywhere, and throughout history's line—loving who we were and what we do enough, to pass it on. I felt ready to give this meaning to the next part of my life. I felt the Universe would help me provide for this new soul, by prizing my work—knowing the things *I* didn't know about parenting, would be shared with me. I knew a deep love in myself—an extra dimension beyond my love for Maleita—a love for what was child-like, tender, and about to bloom—in Michelle, in myself. Wheeeuwh! So be it! Here we go!

Passages

Die to the womb
Hi to the world

Die to the breast
Hi to the feast

Die to the diapers
Hi to the duds

Die to the swing set
Hi to the zits

Die to the family
Hi to the date

Die to the home
Hi to our own

Die to our sleep
Hi to our child

    who has

Died to the womb
Now "hi"s to the world...

No Thanks

He smelled bad. I don't remember his name. He gave me a great gift.

It was getting dusky in D. C. I was walking across campus, on my way back to my quarters, at the Third Order Regular Franciscan House. I still have no idea what Third Order Regular means, outside of a relay shout to the cook at a burger joint. I'm betting it would be a head scratcher for Francis. I was doing dishes there, in return for room and board, while I studied a great variety of philosophers and theologians, in a surprising (to me) place: the Catholic University of America. In the seminaries I had studied in, the "variety" of theologians was basically Thomas Aquinas. And here at C.U. in the mid–sixty's, the trick was *not* to go to the Theology School, but to the Religious Education Department. It was rife with explorers, and comfortable with questions.

The young man with the aggressive fragrance had only one question when he stopped me. "Hey man, you know where I can find a place to bunk down tonight?" I paused, taking in the well-layered road grime, the free-range beard, the lumpy, sagging back pack, and finally—a guitar case. We are probably the same age. Mid–20's. I wonder if I could do what he is doing—winging the primal part of his existence. The guitar gets me. I know I'm going to help. I play.

I tell him, Hey, I don't know. I'm a pretty new student here (2 weeks), and it's not my home town, and I live off campus. But let's see. I think I can guess a building to go to for *info* anyway.

We go, and find out I can sign him in, for a small fee, if he is a family member or close friend. *And all* the dorms currently have open guest rooms. We strike out to the closest of these. I *tell* him I'm a player. He says, "Cool."

We enter the dorm and I knock on the R.A.'s (Resident Assistant's) door and ask about shelter for my new "close friend." He, and two more dorms and R.A.'s, say they have no room. On a hunch, I say wait here to my companion and go to the next dorm alone, and, for the small fee mentioned, I get him a room. As I carry his back pack, which I later learn contains all his worldly possessions, save for what's in the guitar case, we walk up to the R.A., who has the same startled (if not repulsed) look as the others, but it is too late. We're in.

"I need a shower so bad, man," he says, "but if you want to stay a little, you can pull out my axe and play it." He disappears into the bathroom. I open the case. Wow. I probably said it out loud in the room. It is a Martin. A Dreadnought model. The holy grail for a folkie. It is in perfect condition. The interior of the case is plush, immaculate, and just beautiful. I delicately lift out the instrument, make a few small tuning adjustments, and do a few nondescript riffs and strums I usually do on my own guitar, to warm up. The sound is rich and balanced and steel and woody. I am in love.

"Sounds good," he says from the bathroom. "Take your time. I'm washin' out my clothes." When he re-enters the room, in what I assume is his one change of clothes from the back pack, and a trim of the wildest and wooliest regions of his beard, I extend the Martin out to him. He reaches into a compartment in the case, and pulls out a set of finger picks, and I am excited. Everyone I know strums. Few know how to finger pick. To break down in a flow, the elements of the chords, and maybe even include a moving melody, or harmony line. He rips right into *"It ain't no use to sit and wonder why, Babe. If you don't know by now."* The Dylan classic that is not classic yet. His voice is clear and clean, his soul spilling out the song. But as integral as he makes all the elements, I am focused like a laser on the picking style. The minute the song is over I say, *"What* is that picking pattern?"

"Well," he says, "that's basically Travis picking."

"Travis?"

Joe Wise

"Yeah. A player from Kentucky. Merle Travis." He pauses. "Would you like to learn it?"

I say yes with way less enthusiasm on the outside, as I am feeling on the inside. Here I am *from* Kentucky, with a guy I don't know from where, in Washington D.C., being given the key, to a picking style I would use profusely, throughout my as-yet-to-fully-blossom career, which I wasn't seeking anyway. This seems to me the very definition of grace.

He takes his time with me. Patiently, as we hand the guitar back and forth. I tell him I didn't want to keep him up, but I may not be a quick study here. He says, "If you really want it, I won't let you leave the room till you got it."

He didn't and I did. Get it. I tell him goodnight at some a.m. juncture, and literally run to my quarters in glee, tinged with a slight fear, that my neural firings will lose some of this, before it can become, as it did eventually, like breathing. I play it softly on my Gibson on my bed. I play it on my t-shirt as I fall asleep. I play it first thing out of bed. It is mine now. I can't wait to get back to his dorm and room, with my good news. As soon as my early morning dishes are done, I grab up a couple of muffins for us, and dash across campus. Out of breath at the R.A's door, I find out my "close friend," had checked out early, and had moved on.

I walk out, stunned, and disappointed. I have no one to celebrate my triumph with. I sit on the grass, and eat "our" breakfast. This same grassy mall would see me every week, with those I had yet to meet, singing and leading the songs that felt most like my generation: "Where Have All the Flowers Gone, " "Blowin' in the Wind," " If I had a Hammer." Some would be graced by the Travis pick. I suddenly feel the other reason I so want to see my friend. To say thanks.

And so these 47 years later, I send it out: "Wherever you are in this wide universe, and as close as my breathing—"Thanks, man."

No Thanks II

The first time I was in the Library of Congress was not as a tourist taking in a D.C. landmark. I was there as a student. Looking for books available only there. It was pre-Google, pre-Kindle, ride-the-bus-and-open-the-book time. Circa 1965. The following year I would begin frequent correspondence with Department E of this establishment as I began to copyright a steady stream of music and lyric and written word well into the 90's.[7]

This day, though, is given to taking in the enormity and, for me, sacred ambience of this vast edifice given to the humility of not knowing. A place of infinite teachable moments, and unexpected expansions. I have always loved libraries. Thanks to Andrew Mellon, many of us have experienced studying in buildings that had great weight, and personnel who fostered a pervasive and pregnant silence. Louisville, Kentucky, thank goodness, was no exception. I seemed to divide a lot of my youth between the ball field (or court) and the library. I am writing *this* in a relatively small one in a relatively small town in Arizona.

I couldn't wait to see my first congressman (no congresswomen yet, I don't think) come into the Library of Congress. Not that I knew what any of them looked like.

I find a helpful guide and get started on my searches. And researches. The morning and afternoon evaporate into that timeless world of exploration when it's *your* Everest. For me, today, it was several thinkers who got left out of my Catholic education: Teilhard de Chardin, Paul Tillich, Soren Kierkegaard...

My next glance up reveals the time. My bus will leave in fifteen minutes. Just enough time. I had come across town from my quarters at Catholic University of America, where I am in a Masters program. This will be my last bus to get to my transfer point today. I get myself and my satchel squared away and bound down the front steps. My bus is there and I'm quick on board.

On my way toward the back, I see just one place. I'm glad to have it. My ride-mate in this tandem seat looks to be my age, mid-20's. He too had a satchel. Been at the L.O.C.? I want to say in the voice of the most seasoned human and scholar he's ever met. But gratefully I dropped my pretense early in its existence and said: "Student?"

"Yeah."

"Whereabouts?"

"Howard."

"Oh," I say, "I've heard your choir. Knock me out."

"Yeah, they're pretty good."

"Not that I think that's the main thing about a university." I tried to get on better ground. I felt like I had said, "Have you ever seen Muhammad Ali? He can really yodel." I had heard the choir. They elicited, with more classical selections, the same feelings I would later have hearing Ladysmith Black Mambazo. By then, my favorite male soloist was Leon Bibb, and female, Odetta. These were the people I heard consistently coming from inside the song.

"What are you taking?" I get back to balance.

"World History and Social Studies mostly. How about you?"

"Philosophy and Comparative Religions over at Catholic U." It is probably only me who is surprised at how strange that really sounds, after eons of Catholic fear and ignorance, if not arrogance, about other religions. Defining the whole world as Catholic and non.

"Is that where you're going now?" he says.

"Yeah. I got dish duty tonight. It's my job for a place to stay."

He tells me where he is staying while he is getting his degree. How full it is of things his family does not have. How he and they are

D.C. natives but his folks didn't want him to have all the distractions of his home and neighborhood. I get the sense of his being the first and only from his extended family to find himself in such a place. I don't hear pressure. I hear humility and gratitude. And a kind of shyness that *I* feel so familiar with. I feel okay coming back with some of *my* journey to here.

I find an unexpected comfort in a vast new city on a vehicle jammed with strangers.

"You get off at the next stop," he says, attending to my rookie bus route transfer skills. He stands up with me and grabs his book bag.

"Is this where you transfer to Howard too?"

"This corner can get rough sometimes."

A rocket of fear launches itself and suffuses my stomach. What does *that* mean? We get off. It's the same corner I transferred on this morning. There was nobody there then. Looked like nobody now. The day is surrendering its light and apparently its safety.

"Let's go back here," he says and we wedge ourselves in a small entrance to a closed shop. It is closed closed. Empty closed. We have a good view of the whole wide-sidewalked corner. The street lamp is already on. We are more and more shadowed.

The corner begins to fill up.

"What about *your* bus?" I say quietly.

"I'll get back on the same one we were on. It'll get me to my transfer."

The gathering on the corner began to look like storm clouds. Young, angry men. Some jostling. Some language eruptions. Sustained loudness. Some pushing. Jacket weather filled my mind with every possible carry-along. When might *they* come out?

I have not as yet, this very year and the next (in my home town of Louisville), experienced the open housing push and marches, while living in an integrated neighborhood. Not as yet run a neighborhood coffee house where we turned kids with weapons away. Not as yet had it firebombed on the second floor living quarters because we offered it as a place for Martin Luther King to stay while he joined the march. It was one of several secret (we thought) places to give him some measure of safety. He was, thank God, not there.

"Now. Let's go." I hear in a whisper as I see my bus pulling up. He is timing us to get to curbside exactly when the front door opens. A slight push from him and I am on. The door closes, the brakes unhiss, and I am away. In the aisle, I am looking back to see what might happen to…we never got each other's name. The last view I have, he is talking to two or three huge toughs.

O my God, I exhale, and continue silently in prayer for him. His safety. His life opening out during and after world history and social studies. His life opening out after *this night's* history and social studies.

Thank you, my brother.

The J.T. Singers

My friend Mike sent me a program and ad from the 60's for The J. T. Singers, a group of my friends and family who formed around a love to sing. This blossomed into performing. As far as I know, we are all still carrying the "secret" of what J. T. stands for.

Dear Mike,

"Where indeed have they gone?" Referring to, and thanking you for your letter and The J. T. Singers' program from the Stone Age. Almost all are grandparents. One did Viet Nam. One, a kidney transplant (when they were new). One became a Jill-of-all-trades handywoman. All are still *alive*.

What an era. I loved it. I remember, with the warmest heart, sitting under a tree at St. Mary's with you (and your clean, accomplished guitar work) and me (fudging F chords on Charley's Sears Silvertone), belting out the MTA—giving the verse to whoever could remember *that* one. "Did he ever return?..."

I had only recently been smitten (on vinyls, surreptitiously) by Joan Baez and Leon Bibb. The "folk" world was reviving and thriving. It truly felt like it belonged to the people. A great paradigm as I studied in a hierarchic Church. "Irene, Goodnight"—at school year's end at Paca St. (our downtown Baltimore seminary—to Irene, we sang. She who watched all our afternoon games, from her second story windowsill across the street, and kept the neighborhood rowdies, who we never saw, she kept them, by name, throwing our balls back over the big brick wall, whenever they were inclined to do otherwise. Open window, and watching, in all weather. She cried up there as we sang. Both years I was there. I felt infinitely more connected to her and playing ball, than almost anything else inside the walls.

At Roland Park (our suburban school of theology) it felt absolutely conspiratorial to sing with you out on the lawns. "Unholy" worldly songs. Of course they were holy. About the arenas where sacraments most live. In the everyday.

I could not, or chose not to, at some level have all these awarenesses consciously at the time. They went in the slush fund of suppression and "sublimation," along with almost everything else I liked in my life, as I entrusted it to the priests who trained priests.

I can still remember the first time I heard Pete Seeger, and later experienced him. The first in a "live" recording, later in person. Something inside me said *"Here's* my priest." The same way I much later and much more consciously affirmed the same, of James Taylor and Joni Mitchell.

My die was being cast long before I knew it. A moment at the end of a choir rehearsal with Gene Walsh when he walked out, saying: "I have a friend who writes lyrics; if any of you write music you might have a look," dropping a sheath on the table. A surprise discovery from my folk venture: I could play a song without being able to read music—through the chord structure. Could I also compose one this way? I wasn't even slightly tempted to pick up those lyrics, or write my own, with a melody, till sometime later. But that "permission" or assumption that a late-teen seminarian could "write" a song, by Gene, was a powerful seed. Mixed with my "folk birth" and my hanging out with and learning from you—it made for a fine soup down my road.

I thank you for your part in my picture. In the picture. You have been generous. And energetic. And duly "protestful" as every folkie need be.

Where *have* all the flowers gone? The ones we were, in 1960 and beyond. I like to believe our bouquet continues long after our bud has passed.

It was a great garden, and I'm proud to have been in it.

Love,

Joe

Butterfly

I was often asked "Do you get butterflies before you sing?" I could always answer, "Yes." No one ever asked me if I got butterflies playing golf. I did. Once

In my thirties. After a particularly dense and sustained schedule of concerts, retreats, and studio sessions. After a neurologist told me to cut my schedule in half. I asked him when was the last time he had done that. He paused, then asked me what I did to relax. "Ever play golf?"

"I played a little about fifteen years ago. It was hard. And it took a lot of time. Basketball is my thing."

"Does it gear you down?"

"Are you kidding? It revs me completely up."

He was exceptional at letting *me* make his point.

The following week found me at a scheduled school assembly in Frankfort, the capitol of my then home state. I had heard of a particularly beautiful course there, so I threw my clubs in with my guitar and sound system. They looked lost and unpatriated amid the mics and amps, cases and speakers in my van bed. It reminded me of Sesame Street's song, "One of these things is not like the other…" A visual aid, somehow staged by my doc?

First, the assembly. The clubs wait in the van. It goes well. I am off. *On* for the assembly. *Off* for the links.

The course is beautiful. I push through my ecological and sociological hesitations to "be a golfer." The use of land and water, the restrictions of affordability, are not issues I will ponder this glorious Spring Kentucky day. My neurons thank me for that. This is a public course. Green fees are twelve dollars. I get a pull cart for my clubs. I won't have to be hoisting and hefting them all afternoon. More points on my chill chart.

I walk out onto the first tee. It is one of the high points on the course. I see the immense and varied lushness of southern grasses and greenery. I smell the honeysuckle and take in the flashes of red and yellow and purple and orange from the petals of the color guard surrounding me on the tee box.

I am playing alone. Part of this is to eliminate any anxiety I may have, regarding a display of my current skills. Part of it is, I am comfortable playing alone. Sometimes I prefer it.

I am surprised, in a good way, by my first tee shot. Beginner's luck? Certainly a "no thought" swing. Natural. Lessons abound. I slide my driver into the bag and stride off down the fairway. Nobody behind me. Somebody on me. Some thing. I see it has a body. Supporting two of the most beautiful wings. A butterfly on my shoulder. I don't break stride.

I arrive at my ball and stop. He (?) hop-flutters to my right, ungloved, hand. I say hello. Out loud. To this flying kaleidoscope I hold in front of my face. He flutters. "You are looking great today." Flutter. I tell him he'd do better on my bag for what comes next, and extend him and my hand next to it. He hops on. I then pull out a club, take a practice swing, and then a "real" one. I am pleased with the result, and return the club to the bag. My now-companion then flies to my shoulder, and we move on toward the green. When I stop, he flies to the bag. I chip and putt. More often than I want. He stays on my bag, off the green, almost twenty yards away.

We had begun the rhythm of our nine holes. At the end of each, he would fly to my hand or finger and not to my shoulder. We would commune, me still speaking out loud. And any time I said anything about his beauty and his wings, he would fan them down and full out. I can't help but be aware of how slow, and sometimes embarrassed I am, to shine. Presently, I would move him and my hand next to my shoulder. He would hop on and return his wings to

Joe Wise

their "full upright and locked position" for his new mode of travel, me. He chose not to do any freelance flying for the two hours we shared. I was leaving after nine holes. Eighteen was an option. Would he know?

I came off the last green and stood by my bag. He didn't come to my shoulder or finger. Instead he flew all around me. Top to bottom. Bottom to top. Front to back. I held out my hand. He lighted. I said good-bye. There were repeated swishes of wings and "holds" for my admiration. Then he lifted off. I watched till I could no longer see him.

I have no recollection of how well or poorly I played golf that day, except for the opening hole, which I played both well *and* poorly. I *do* have great recollection of how *present* I was, how timeless, how teachable, thanks in great measure to my nameless messenger/model with the magnificent wings.

Do I get butterflies when I play golf? No. But, once, I got one. And he got *me*.

★   ★   ★

I don't frequent butterfly-rich environments here in Arizona. They are a rare sighting for me. The morning before I began writing this piece, I was wing-kissed on the leg, by a solo butterfly passing through, as I entered my run at Windmill Park in Cornville. He was quite large, with intense yellow and black wings.

The morning after I finished writing this piece, I was wing-kissed on the chest, on the heart, briefly, by a solo butterfly passing through, as I began my run in Cottonwood, *miles* from Cornville's park, on a synthetic track, around a synthetic football field, fenced in from everything natural. He was quite large, with intense yellow and black wings. I said out loud through my smile, "You're welcome."

Reading *Out on a Limb*

I took this topic from one of my lists of "pivotal events" in my life.

There's still a trace of shame in saying this was my portal into my current place with matters of the Spirit. It would feel much more heroic and noble and sophisticated, to say it was reading the *Upanishads,* or the *Bhagavad Gita,* or the works of Lao-tzu. No, Shirley MacLaine was my priestess, my midwife—she got me through the door. Where I went on to travel into and with—Joel Goldsmith, Ramana Maharshi, Papaji, Sai Baba, Gangaji, Yogananda, Eckhart Tolle, and ultimately the Stillness, the Silence.

It was a journey that witnessed my letting go of a need for Redemption, of a need for any God *outside* myself. Taking charge of my own spiritual (and isn't it all) life. Letting go of guilt and shame as primary religious ingredients, and welcoming everything to satsang, or truth session, truth awareness. Meanwhile owning I am capable of extreme thoughts and feelings, recognizing them as human, welcoming them and discovering, I don't have to act on them. I can own and express my anger, rage even, without hurting myself or anybody else.

This journey is radically different from anyone else among my old family-and-friends circle. To begin it, felt horribly disloyal to them. Taking enormous courage. It felt so true to do, so I did.

Allowing myself to question in a realm I had been so secure

in—studying 10 years to be a Roman Catholic priest—the surest of the sure.

What would I do? Who would I go to? I started Church-hopping. Liked the Quakers the best. Lots of silence. Direct communion. Revelation to all is listened to. Including children. Reminding me weekly, concretely, how gender-blind and age-blind God, Truth, is. Found Joel Goldsmith or at least a living student of his, Frank Martin. Let myself be fostered.

Opened to the Eastern mystics. My soul *and body* are feeling more and more relaxed. *Nobody* is excluded. No doctrines. No separation from the Divine, *ever*. Only a sometimes *sense* of separation. I will never again have to be good to get God. Great relief.

I feel a certain sense of admiration for myself—heading out into virgin territory—virgin to me and, as far as I knew, to *all* of my friends. Not one encouraged me. I feared a rift with many. It only happened with a few. I felt powerful to stand in my own Spiritual truth, outside the circle of the established religions. I began to recognize that all religions have a mystical dimension. It obscures the easiest among the rules, and fears of extinction. It celebrates the direct connection with the Divine—which lessens an institution's necessity.

I rejoice for the freedom I feel in this arena. I thank myself for the brave beginning. *And* I thank Shirley.

Kahlil

They had come from leagues around

oceans around

hemispheres around

this unlikely grouping –

herring, shark, bass,

flounder, salmon, and whale,

minnows to behemoths

sleek river runners

to sea bottom sledgers

all of a mind

all of a spirit

to this most hallowed sage

this most revered of all the masters

Kahlil of the Carp.

"Master, Master"

the chorus arose

"we are looking for God."

The word–bubbles ascended

and popped.

Kahlil watched them vanish

up, up to the last,

brought down his gaze

to the throngs

adjusted his wire frames

and cleared his ancient gills

"Very well"

(he spoke with such grace)

"we'll attend to that presently.

But first and before everything

we will all go out

in search of water."

Laughter

laughter

everywhere laughter.

Kahlil smiles

"School's out."

★   ★   ★

Or as Martin Buber put it: "There is no such thing as seeking God, for there is nowhere He cannot be found."

Hamstring Tear

Name 5 defining moments in your life. My pen kept going to 11. This leaves me 10 other topics.
1. *Getting sober*
2. *Marrying Maleita*
3. *Having Michelle and John*
4. *Going to seminary*
5. *Leaving the seminary*
6. *Death of John Wirth*
7. *Picking up guitar*
8. *Changing careers*
9. *Moving to Sedona*
10. *Taking drawing class at 52*
11. *Hamstring tear*

What a blow. What a shock. I am in my early forties, and this is my first major injury. I call it major now because of how long it persisted and how wide was its effect. I had many sprains, black eyes, bruises, scrapes. They were all visible—the sprains by the wraps or the crutch. They all carried a visible call for sympathy. A ready signal to others why my behaviors might change, and I might be less capable on the physical world. Or badges of participation. Scrapes and bruises happen only to those who engage in the game. I was a brave one.

I was reaching into the dryer for my clothes and it snapped. It was loud. I've met a few others who had tears, not strains. They all were amazed by the sound. The doctor said, "Don't challenge it for 6 months." Months, not weeks. He mentioned a few no-no's. I discovered all the rest. The rest that kept me from my sports for 3 years. It was a horrendous withdrawal. I also looked bad. Not physically. You couldn't see it. I could feel it. The shape of my hamstring on my right leg, was noticeably altered compared to my left. I remember getting so mad at my body and the injury, I ran up a hill pulling a lawn mower, way too heavy for recovery. It was one of dozens of re-injuries—most a surprise, some in deliberate rage. Surprises were heavy grocery bags, stuck windows, heavy doors, my suitcases.

I had to ask for help in a million ways, if I wanted to proceed. It was humbling. With no visible injury, I go through an airport with my wife, or a host, carrying *all* the luggage. None had sprouted wheels yet. I begged for an operation. The orthopede said, "We tear as much as we put together. Go for natural healing." I was re-injuring myself in my sleep, the unkindest cut of all. Natural shifts in bed became a menace. I had to keep myself semi-awake all night. My usual releases were evaporating—basketball and running. Only alcohol gave me release now.

As I look back, I see I was at the beginning of a huge change in my life. I was preparing to let go of a career in writing music, recording, and performing because it was beginning to be over, turning out my lights. The hamstring is the largest muscle in the body for moving forward, and lifting or picking up things. I see now it was helping my psyche act, decide, move on. I did not want to go forward with my life in that career. Nobody else, I thought, would understand. I didn't either at the time.

I felt at the other end of powerful. Physically, psychically. It infected all the rest of my self. I drank more. The torn hamstring wouldn't go away. Many people I loved began to die. It was a dark time for me.

It was an amazing catalyst. I am so grateful I hung on, and

Joe Wise

decided to go on—even not knowing what, if anything, I would do next. I am grateful to that part of myself, that stepped toward light and life—however gingerly, with a torn hamstring.

And then the rest of me—slowly followed.

My Eulogy

This piece was born in my journal group. We took turns hosting and presenting springboards for exploration. This invitation was to write your own eulogy for the service.

He played with matches as a kid. Was an adventurer on his bike. Pushed the envelope of boundaries on three, then two wheels. Seldom told his parents where he had been, lest those destinations be removed from his itineraries.

Displayed a notable penchant for sports at an early age, which he continued right up to the end—as he keeled over on his desk, shooting a paper wad at the waste basket. He missed by the way.

His mental acumen was legendary, often remembering up to 3 items with no list at Safeway. He proved quite astute in choosing a spouse.

He fathered and fostered two children who have spoken to him continuously to his last day—freely, about the root things in their life, with all the feelings that go with such revelations.

Somewhere in his 40's he made a series of profoundly courageous choices. To let go of booze. To let go of organized religion (which had fed his coffers and his egoic needs). To let go of the jobs that singled him out in the world as a unique public contributor. To wander through the dark bardo, seeking re-engagement with something that would feel true to his soul.

He picked up the pen again, and omitted the music, and chose to use it this time as a shovel, and a compass, into the wealth of the many years of experience he had accumulated. Not all of it appeared as wealth on the surface. Often laced with pain and darkness. Embracing himself from the 7 directions. North, South, East, West, Above, Below, Within. The hero's journey.

With tools from Richard Simmons and Daniel Smith—not the weight loss or cough drop fellows[8]—he plunged into the world of color—some would even say "off color"—but these are people who are not truly acquainted with Duochrome Hibiscus, or Indanthrone Mauve. Since then he left a paper trail of Arches[9] that extends over quires and quires,[10] finding this unique way of returning to music.

He had the good sense in his 50's and 60's to open his heart and his life to Golden Retrievers—realizing it was only the dyslexics who really knew who Dog was. He abandoned his car, and his clothes, and his face freely to their ministrations, and considered this his lasting testimonial to personal wisdom.

In a similar fit of sagacity, he moved to Sedona, and surrendered all his belongings to red dust.

To the very end he invoked heaven and hell over his three iron, took inordinate glee at outcomes on the *Justice Files*, and rued the anatomical design that did not allow for unlimited Breyer's.

To his utmost credit, and perhaps his finest achievement, he learned how to achieve stillness.

I mean, look at him!

Alicia, Letter of Unfinished Business

Periodically, leading my group sessions in various treatment centers, I would invite us to write a letter to someone with whom we had unfinished business. Most often, this would involve an unresolved conflict, or a known, but as yet "unvoiced" issue. I offered an expansion to include a teacher, or friend, you haven't "thanked" enough, and even a letter to a little one about your future hopes. As with everything you write in a journal of this kind, it is meant for your eyes and heart only. However, once written, you can make a decision about whether to mail it, or share it.

I'm saving this one for Alicia, my granddaughter, (8, going on 30) for a little while longer. Maybe when she's 12. Maybe next week

Dear Alicia,

You are just over 7 months. You teethe. You flail your dolls. You come just shy of an insurance claim with your spoon. You flip over naked, before the change. I know all of these things from your Mom, who describes them to me over the phone. You are 830 miles from my heart. I have seen you physically only three times for a total of 20 days. It is not enough for me. This is hard.

You have chosen a killer couple for your launch. Michelle and Tim are so dialed in. You are laying, and now sitting, on a bed of love.

Most of what's unfinished between us, I hope, is in the future. I want to be with you at least once in silence when the sun sets. Walk in the hills of Colorado or Sedona with the flowers. Sit across a table from you and receive your day. Laugh with you at something silly I have done—on purpose, and not. Hold you in my arms or on my shoulders while my frame will still be able. Come to see you *do* anything or nothing. Share an ocean walk. I will be keen to notice what unique flash and bouquet you bring to the jeweled and flowered offerings in the world.

I will love to draw with you and push paint around and create things and show-and-tell them. I will await the time you can speed dial me and say English words we'll both know. I love all the ones on the way, right now.

I do so wish I could be more of the beginning imprint and interaction circle you are fostered with. As fully as I wish I could often, and at will, receive the benedictions of all your early wisdom and clarity and directness.

My favorite picture of us is large and on the closest thing to a mantle in my house. It is in the *living* room. Where I live most of the time. I pass it, you, on the way to everywhere I go—in and out of the house. I usually say "hi Alicia" as I go past. It is a close up of your face. Your hands are full of, and tugging at, my hair. Only my hair and a little of my forehead are in the picture. Your face is lost in delight. Your eyes rolled to the side. A relaxed grin and a tiny tongue escaping sideways from your mouth. This picture is a perfect picture of my feelings about being and not being able to be more physically in your life. All of you seems there. Just a little of me is there. My title for this picture deflects my sadness at my geographic absence. I call it. "Easy, it's all I got."

When you're old enough to grasp male patterned baldness, you'll get this.

I do so want to live long enough for that to bring an extra smile to your face. It will mean we can communicate in new dimensions. We will have a history. We will be as we are today—two souls lucky enough to get on this trip together. We'll just have a lot more to talk about in the locker room.

Love,

Papa

Joe Wise

The Price

The price of right

of being right

is getting way too high.

I find

I'm springing for it

less and less

these days.

Free Wheeling

"You wanna throw some clay?"

"Uh, yeah."

"You wanna throw some pots, some mugs, vases and cups?"

"Heck yeah."

How disappointed I was to find out throwing, had nothing to do with hurling brittle objects against a stone wall, to hear them crash, and watch them shatter. Or even to take wet clay and fast ball a blob into a pancake on a wall. Clocked his clay at 92 miles per hour. Red Sox scout in lab impressed.

I *love* to throw things. I loved it as a kid. I still do. I'm especially fond of throwing things with no objective. No strike zone. No pass receiver. I get enough targeting from shooting hoops daily. Supplemented by paper wads to the trash can, keys to my wife upstairs, coins to the tollbooth funnel. The part I don't get enough of is just random and/or break something throwing.

It was a real let down, when I found out the clay workshop for teachers involved *forming* clay, not really throwing it like the brochure said/or asked. Well you did throw it *once*—when you put your wedge on the wheel. If I got it right, wedge is both what you do to your clay to prepare it to be thrown, and the result of what you do. I got my first hunk of clay and began to wedge it. The instructor/ potters wedged theirs, leaning into the table. Mine was really more randomly kneaded. Theirs began to take shape like a conical seashell. Mine looked a lot like Freddy Krueger.[11]

The object they told me, was to knead all the air holes out of the clay. In a kiln, an air hole explodes the whole piece. Would this be like the clay throwing itself, or at least throwing in the towel? My lump…unh…my wedge is just a little bigger than my hand, and they say, "Now pick it up and start smacking it." I say, "What do you mean?" Tom, the tallest co-leader, says, "I smack it thirty times, but never in the same place twice. I say, "Oh, it's like golf."

Immediately I notice how many upper body muscles snap to attention—ones I apparently don't use, when I work out every other day on the universal, over at the gym. I glance up and notice Tom and John (the other instructor). Rippling arms. Rolled-up sleeves. I make a mental note to never arm wrestle a potter for anything important.

This is a day for teachers. Sponsored by the Kentucky Art Educators Association. And there is one teacher in this workshop and two walk ons. My wife and I are the walk ons. The teacher is at the intermediate level. Maleita threw twenty years ago. Today I am breaking my maiden. Great. I do get to break something.

The instructors take their beautifully formed candy kiss wedges with rounded bottoms, and throw them on their wheels. I'm still not ready. Tom cut my wedge in half with a wire, revealing several air holes on the inside. I push and pull my wedge again on the table, smack it thirty times till it's at least an upside-down candy corn, if not a Hershey's Kiss, and fire that sucker right on to my wheel. It hits way off center. They had said to throw it on the center. I missed considerably, even though my release was only inches away from the wheel. I think, well, I better pick it up and throw it again. It doesn't come off in a piece—the bottom part is real stuck to the wheel. I will have to do another wedge. John is already forming a bowl. Maleita has found center. John *and* Tom could have made a table setting by now.

I come up with a wedge more Kiss-like this time. I invoke the spirit of Cy Young to help me get this one down the middle. It happens. I look around. Nobody has noticed. I watch and listen to John tell Maleita how to raise the clay, and push it back down several times, to fine tune the centering. Her wheel is spinning. I don't see how. I walk around. She's standing on one leg and pushing a lever back and forth with the other. She looks like an exceptionally coordinated flamingo. I walk back to my side and get the wheel going. I wet my hands and cup them wedge-like around the clay, and begin to raise it up. Wow. It works. And then push it down with the palm of one hand, keeping it centered and rounded with the other. The first thing I notice is mine is getting all teeter-tottered, and quite unconical. John immediately says, "Would you like me to help you center it?" Oh, I think, staying centered goes on forever. He says, "I think I can save it for you." I am not proud. "Please."

He re-centers me. It is the first of many acts of assistance I will receive in the next two hours, en route to producing nothing. Somewhere in the heart of the session I say, "Hey Maleita."

"Yeah."

"That man we bought the dishes from in New Mexico?"

"Yeah."

"We didn't give him a nickel too many."

"Yeah."

Everybody's work is in progress. Wheels are humming. Pots are forming. Vases climbing. I find a rhythm of my own. Wedge, throw, re-center, destroy. Wedge, throw… Oh, and clean the wheel. I learn a lot about cleaning the wheel.

I am beginning to feel at home with the goo and the wet and the bulk of the clay. I remember games in the mud. Football games in the mud with my friends at Victory Park. Games with no names in the mud. As clean as I've kept myself as an adult, I begin to revel in the mess. It is on my shirt and pants. My beard, my shoes. I am in the mud and the mud's in me.

I *thank* the clay, and I am thanking me. My friend Clayton Kua, from the big island of Hawaii, told me how he spoke to Madam Pelee, the goddess of the volcano, long and lazy one hot Sunday afternoon, before he took her lava rock to build his fireplace. He thanks her every time he lights a fire there. I remember scenes in books I read, where Apache and Navajo gather to thank the spirit of the buffalo for the gift of his life and hide.

I thank my clay for letting me play with it, fume with it, wrestle with it. I still have fresh muscle memory, of the balance of strength and grace it takes, to hollow out and raise a wall of clay. Much dialogue. I wonder how it felt, my wedge, spinning on my wheel, light years faster than on its *terra firma* axis.

Tomorrow at the gym, I will remind myself, to thank the tree that throws my basketball back to me, each time I bounce it on her flanks.

Today I thank my child, for calling me to play with clay. I thank my adult, for the courage to answer the call, and risk a poor performance. My adolescent, for the strength and drive to stay the course. My soul, for finding me a spirit guide in my life, to help me re-center, time after time after time. And all of me, for writing a piece so freewheeling.

I am going to have to go out now, and find the biggest rocks in my driveway, and throw them high and hard into the dark woods.

The Arizona Cowboy

In journal group, the leader presented a "deck" of recently collected images, face down. We all drew two, chose one, and wrote. One of my two was of a 50's poster with the words "The Arizona Cowboy" at the top, and an illustration of a man named Rex Allen. I thought I knew of all the singing cowboys. I didn't. Billed as the last of the singing cowboys, he did about 20 movies in the mid-50's. And he lived in Arizona. Being myself a singer, and a fairly recent transplant, along with my lifelong love of, and admiration for, Roy Rogers, my choice was easy.

The Arizona Cowboy. That's me. 8 1/2 years ago. Coming from Kentucky. Not entirely bootless. But hatless. And I still remain gunless. I slacked off the boots big time, after a running injury. They don't allow for sustained natural stretching. Still wear them on occasion. Got the hats. Two of them. I find I'm not wearing them very much. I'm finding clothes don't make the cowboy. Reminds me of the widower from Texas, line-dancing with a friend of mine, assessing a man across the room on the make, and pronouncing him "All Hat and No Cattle."

There are few professions we've romanticized more. I remember how shocked I was the first time I saw how brief was the cowboy era in this country. My childhood, like everybody's, was forever—so I assumed the era that had Roy, Gene, and Hopalong, or their real counterparts, was almost endless.

I guess what keeps it alive is the *spirit* of the cowboy. Loner. Sufficient. One with the animal and nature world. Equally capable of engaging in frontier love, as he was in frontier justice. Somebody willing to lean hard on his own inner resources. A monk of the plains. A Zen master of the foothills. Equestrian Buddha.

I already felt myself a cowboy in Kentucky. I was on a road less traveled. Blazing some trails. Guitar as weapon of choice. Music as ammunition. And campfire comfort. Working a profession not linked with the common.

There is something eternally intriguing to me about being a contrarian. It helps me stay my course. Part of it is, for sure, a crippling (as far as peace goes) dictum I internalized unconsciously, in childhood and beyond: "I must be special or I can't belong." A very powerful motivator, combined with my sense of "that's not true—this is, and I'll show you why, or invite you to look again." Unblessed by any authority but the rightness of the feeling.

I still find myself looking for the unusual, the forgotten, the underestimated, the abandoned. Cowboy genetics. Championing the natural, the intuitive, the independent. Now, I'm also open to not depriving myself of the comfort, of coming in from the range sometimes, and sitting down at the table with the Eastern bankers and bakers, politicos and petticoats, regular folk. Owning my "regular" part. But seldom staying for dessert.

Conversations with Muli

Yesterday I heard someone on NPR say, "What would your dog say about your life and the way you are living it?" This is my response.

I have a grand-dog, a golden retriever. His name is Mulligan. He belongs to Charlie and Jan Lundstrom, and they belong to him. They move back and forth between Michigan and Arizona. While here in Arizona, I get to spend time with Mulligan frequently, including our five-mile runs.

Going to see Mulligan produces an anticipation in me equaled by few other events. When he sees, hears, or senses me, he leaps, he barks, he moans, he rolls (slight pause), he leaps, barks, licks, bumps, and yelps. At the end of our run, he sits and holds my gaze for the longest, quiet time. He moves from exuberance to Buddha-like stillness easily and swiftly.

In golf, his name means grace, another chance, perspective. He carries his name well.

★ ★ ★

Mulligan, please tell me any observations you have about my life.

OK. You don't need anything—you just think you do. Consider the lilies.

You have a lot of hurry in your life. You're not gonna get it all in—and that's not a bad thing. It's a relief.

I see you're catching on to the "nap thing."

You see many things as interruptions. Just re-framing that one thing will bring you much peace.

Never, under any circumstances, deprive yourself of "biscuits"—for the tummy, for the eyes, for the heart.

Don't go "away" when you're here. You can't really anyway.

Check out that drive to Sedona from the Village. Let go of agendas that won't happen till you stop the car.

Take your shoes off more.

Don't breathe in short pants. Just walk in them.

Drop the word "own" and the chain that comes with it, with the possible exception of one very large bone.

Wrestle and bark more. Get into your fierceness. It doesn't have to hurt anybody. And it's a personal rush.

Don't worry so much about your ears going up. Giving away your true position on things is just that—a gift. It's one less bone to guard too.

Pay a lot of attention to comings and goings. Get up and hug or lick or whatever feels right at both junctures—you can nap in between if you want.

If there's a choice between dirty and clean, wet and dry, shaking off or stillness, go for the dirty, wet, shake every time. You can nap in between if you want.

Joe Wise

*Let go of "work" and "play" and have everything be "stuff-you-do."
I'm partial to wagging and gnawing myself.*

*Make friends with beings who can throw things, and will—sticks, love,
parties.*

Companion yourself when they are busy.

*Make your mark on the earth and rest in the coolness you have dug
into.*

Come on over and see me right now.

I'm on my way. Anything else?

Yes. Do one thing. A cell phone in the produce is counterproductive.

Observe the young. Be curious.

If it feels good, moan. (See ears, above).

Chase things with great energy. Surrender fully if they're faster.

*If people show a penchant for petting, roll right over and give them a shot
at your belly too.*

*To truly judge a situation, see what it smells like. This is a highly
underrated procedure.*

If you like somebody and don't want them to leave, sit on their feet.

*Relax. Now is how. Get into it. Stop running from it, and it happens.
Forget wait. It takes you out of now.*

OK, Muli, is that all?

Vita Bones are on aisle six.

I'll see you soon.

★　★　★

And I do. In Charlie's living room. Next to Charlie's chair. With the throw pillow that says, "My goal in life is to be the person my dog thinks I am."

A Talk to 8th Graders at Confirmation

Given at St. Peter's Parish to the students from Butler Catholic School in Butler, Pennsylvania.

What are you going to be when you grow up? I always wanted to say—the same as I am right now—a human being. What am I going to *do* with my life and energy? I now know that's a better way to phrase the question. When I was little, I hated people asking me that question all the time. One of the reasons was I never had an answer, and I always felt like a failure if I couldn't answer a question. A lot of my playmates and classmates already knew what they were going to do when they grew up.

I was so envious. I wanted to be clear. To be sure. It didn't happen for me—making a choice—till I was 11. In my child's mind I decided I wanted to be a priest. It was something everybody liked. I liked a lot of priests I knew. I thought it would be cool to see if I could live away from my family nine months of the year, starting next year. I'd get to be the star in what people did every week (go to Mass). I could help people in between. *And* I'd get a lot closer to God.

I couldn't date and get married, but I wouldn't have to go to war. My job would be secure for my whole career. I'd always have a place to stay and a place to eat. And people would treat me special, especially in public. In return, I'd put them in my prayers. I wouldn't get to play high school or college sports against other schools, but they played all the sports inside the walls and gyms and fields of the seminary. Even track and field I had heard.

They put on plays, had speech and writing contests, and none of this would cost my parents anything. The other Catholics *and* my parents gave their money to the Church, and all the Churches paid for the seminary.

So at age 12 I had a grown-up event. I went away to the seminary. I know getting my license at 16 will be another, and my draft card at 18, and qualifying for liquor buying at 21. This seems to be what America offers as rites of passage or markers for my ascending into adulthood.

As I look at these from now, I wish there had been something more personal, more spiritual, or something in front of the larger community to mark my passage. I was 10 when I got confirmed by the Church. It was in Latin. I didn't get it. I mean I got it, but I didn't get it. *Your* picture looks different as far as this goes. Cool.

And, what do you want to do on the world? What job would you like? Ideally I would hope each of you would be still enough with yourself, tune out as much as you can everybody's expectations of you, or ideas for you, and see what it is you really love to do. What gets your juices going? What engages you? What makes time go away? What you would do if you got paid for it *or not*? *Then* look at what the world needs or ways you think you could help.

Try on the idea of being the star. Try on the idea of being the star's helper. Give yourself total permission to be either. This takes courage. Many, if not all, of the big people in our lives will push for the star. Disappointing an adult who is meaningful in my life will last a while. Disappointing myself may last a lifetime. I need to be ok being the quarterback, the center, the water boy. The leading lady, her dresser, the ticket-taker at the movies. I can change my mind along the way.

I left the seminary. I learned to play guitar. I wrote music, recorded it, gave concerts, got married, have two children, soon a grandbaby. I stopped the music, and now I am a painter, a writer and a teacher. These were not easy, simple transitions for me. I *did* make them, staying true to what keeps my lights on. Some of these changes were as hard as first deciding what to do with my life. People expected me to *always* be a singer and recording artist. I disappointed many. Some told me directly. I loved them for telling me. It wouldn't be a silent divider between us.

Ultimately, people who care about us are happy if *we* are—even if it's by a path they wouldn't have picked for us.

For some of you, going into what you're going to do with your life will be easy and seamless. For many, it's cloudy and jerky and stutter steps. I have a suggestion for all of you. Interview the adults in your life. Call them up. Make an appointment, or just bring it up while you're raking leaves together. Ask them how they ended up doing what they're doing. Was it always clear? Is it what they wanted first? Did they *settle* for something? Did they think they disappointed any adults in *their* lives by what they chose to do? Did they change their mind in midstream, midcareer? If they could do it over, what would they choose?

Lastly, I'd like to say: the world we're handing on to you is not the way I pictured it would be when I began "my watch." My generation and I have had our shot at the world for over forty years. I'm disappointed at how little we seem to have influenced change. We still do wars. We still have rich and poor. We still have people starve. I apologize to you, from us, for our failures.

I celebrate the individual things we've done to make the planet a little more aware, our little circles a better place to be. I don't feel finished yet with my world work. I am, among other things, teaching others, a few at a time, how to gain clarity, release, insights, and blessings for themselves by picking up a pen and writing from their soul. It is rich, rewarding work. I will do it side by side with your work for a while, proud to be a companion of yours. And then it will be completely your turn.

I will pledge my intention to you, to be open and amazed and nurtured by *your* gifts to the world. I will look for you on the playing field, in the offices and hospitals, at the ticket-taker's spot in the theater, on the screen, behind the wheels, in the stores and on the building sites, with the forests and the animals—no less than the trees and the stars, you have a right to be here. You are a child and a man and a woman of the universe. I celebrate your coming of age.

Joe Wise

Ministering to Me

This piece was generated by a question in journal group. "What do you do to take care of yourself?"

Taking care of myself. Ministering to myself. I do this like I do most things. Some I come to on my own. Though this particular enterprise is hard to come by on my own because it wasn't taught to me with any great frequency or urgency. I chalk this up to being only a generation or so past the frontier days. Where everything was geared to group survival, not individual nurturance, certainly not self-nurturance.

Learn to cook, shoot, find water, and sleep with one eye open. Exploring your inner landscape, your emotions, your hidden motivations, your needs and desires was a luxury these hearty souls passed on to *us*. Without instructions. Unwittingly, mostly.

As I have looked around me for models of how to be post-frontier, I have in my 40's, 50's and now 60's looked to people who look pretty comfortable in their own skin. People whose presence I like to be in. For the most part they are vulnerable, laugh easily, welcome sustained silences, and don't spend even a thimble full of energy trying to "fix" me.

I am thinking of Gene Walsh—a priest who taught me Ed. Psych in college. First day of class—class size—near a hundred. He says, "Plato says a man reaches maturity at age 50." My hand shoots in the air. "What do *you* say?" Slight pause. "I don't know. I'm 48. Come back in two years." I was in love. Out of 2 bachelors' and 2 masters' worth of studies—he was, by far and away, my truest teacher. The one I connected with the most. The one who led me out (*educare*) the most.

In his latter years, he and I did many a workshop and convention together. A great privilege for us both. When I wrote a book, he sent me a card saying how much he liked it, and that he was moved to write his own first book. He wrote a half dozen.

People whose presence I love to be in. Eric Wehder. About seven years older. Direct. Speaks what is on his mind. Takes himself seriously. Takes himself with laughter. He has trusted his angry self to me. He goes quickly to the seat of it and aims it where it truly lies. He sits in the woods. He tells stories of bravery on himself. He tells stories of abject shame and many that fall in between. He lets me get to know him. He waits to see if I share back before he gets a little more naked. He'll do some things people would call anti-social, like not going to a lot of parties—*and* he'll call you and tell you he's not coming, and why. He has a large child. He often thinks like a child. He often speaks directly, like a child. Going for the heart or the humor or the pathos or all three. When I get letters from him— often—I see what he is doing to take care of himself, and I imitate *that*. And I add on my own things in the same spirit.

He doesn't see any of this as selfish. It is *my* turn he sometimes says. He remains generous to others. But for my money, the greatest thing he gives any of us who are lucky enough to know him, is the gift of taking care of himself. He leads an examined life. Triggered by current events or movies or books or his own ruminations on his own experiences and life.

What do I do to minister to me?

A lot of little things. Some big. Big, are quiet, away times. Mixed in with people-time. Balance. Little are giving myself this Pilot V Ball grip extra fine point pen to write with, paying extra for Mentadent because my mouth likes it best, taking a nap, and having a current favorite seasonal fruit around.

I have discovered my life truly takes place a day at a time. So if even one day goes by without me giving myself some treats (that only I would know in many cases), I begin to feel deprived and low-level frustrated and not ready to beam much of anything to anybody else.

Slim Goodbody—who my kids loved—the guy with a body leotard that looked like veins and organs—the inside of the body—used to always say, "Food is *the* fuel." My kids said it for years. "Food is the fuel." I *still* say it—four hours into an all-day drive.

Whatever food is to me, whatever Eucharist is to me—whatever sustains and refreshes my body and soul—it is, I now believe, absolutely up to me to look after, and get, and consume or do, all the while staring that big bad word SELFISH right in the eye.

I take best care of those around me by taking best care of myself. You want me when I'm giving you the *second* piece of the pie. Not the first. Burp.

I Used to Think

I used to think

I had to

constantly

be a better version

of me

before God would

really love me.

Now I remind myself

I don't have to believe everything

I think.

Dear Alicia, Letter to a Favorite Teacher

Dear Alicia,

How I wish our time together was longer and more often. Denver is far. I love when you call. I love when we talk. Your word vocabulary is up to pairs now: "our car," "fire truck," " play Papa." When you woke up, you used to stand up in your crib and say "Mama." Now you stand up and say "cereal," "eggs." The morning menu.

I love how you "do" the world. Your powerful walk. Your direct requests for what you want. How many ways you say my name; Paaapa. PAPAA. Not afraid to reveal where you are by the tone and volume. Ready to play. Wanting to be held. Nodding off. Listening to the sound of your own voice.

When you were almost walking, I loved how you crawled over to my legs—used them as steadying poles and almost pull my shorts off while my hands were full, to get me to put down whatever and pick *you* up.

I loved being the point and click Papa during that time. Pointing me to some treasure in the room that was now at your height in my arms and my silent click to "open that window" for you by going there.

Your universe was in *this* room, whichever room you found yourself in. Present. Present. And more present. Be here now. What a gift to me. At this moment I am your focus. Or this book. Or these Legos. What a gift I can offer others. By being truly present. Saying concretely—of all the people and places I could be present to—even in my attention and awareness, people and places *outside* this room and *other* than you—I choose to be here, now. With you.

How often I've seen that vague look in somebody's eye that says "I'm gone." "I'm leaving you now." "I'm not *really* here." "I've got to take this call."

What great grace when we become present to each other, as you have to me. Moving beyond the fear of silence—the discomfort of intimacy—"feel the fear and do it anyway." You remind me so clearly these are the deposits and withdrawals of great treasure.

I love to watch you stare. Unashamedly at persons or things. Truly looking. Aware you *can* look—and see. Sometimes vacantly stare. Aware of your own beingness—even with eyes wide open.

I love to watch you pick up things and examine them. Taste them. Turn them. Throw them. A willingness to be surprised. The very best of the attitude of learning.

I like how free you are to ask for physical comfort. You remind me how essential physical contact, with some frequency, is an equalizer, in a world that buffets me with many things.

I love to watch you sing and dance. Separate or together. You do both like nobody's watching. Accessing your own inner joy in movement and sound. I love how off key your "do do dooh's" are.

My favorite dance of yours so far was the one you did at the Casa Bonita with the mariachi band. Strapped in your chair. Waving your tortilla over your head.

I am at your table of learning. I am reinforced with the biggies.

Hey, Punkin',

Papa

★ ★ ★

I've had several favorite teachers so far, and discovered they are not limited by age, gender, or even species. Some died before I was born. Some have been events, including the unpleasant ones. Those tend to be especially rich lessons and letters.

Prayer

A one-word invitation in journal group.

"Prayer," Leonard Cohen says, "is man translating himself into the language of a child, asking for all that is."

Sebastian Temple sings: "Where shall we hide the truth from man?" A quandary in the conclave of gods who want to begin and maintain lordship. After all seeming possibilities are offered and nixed—one says, "Let's hide it in his heart. He'll never find it there." Bingo.

Even when these two insights were penned, back when "man" stood for "women" too, I knew there was some connection pivotal to how I would relate to what I couldn't see.

My early prayer life, completely taught, zero percent intuited, was asking. Asking nice, but asking. Huge result: feeling and reinforcing my need. I was also taught answering depended on my behavior. Get good, get God, get what you want. Stay bad, get nothing. Then a nuance—I could be good and *not* get what I want, because God thought it wouldn't be good for me. This removed a lot of incentive for prayer. *My* control was compromised. Now I could say the perfect prayer and still have it flop.

There were other prayers than asking ones. Prayers of praise—but as a child I only did those to sweeten the pot and soften the grid for my asking ones.

My understanding of prayer as a child was also irrevocably infused with my Dad and World War II.

God was a father. Not a mother. I much preferred the way my Mom dealt with me and the world, as opposed to Dad's way. *And if* God was in charge of the world, and all the big people in my life affirmed that *He* was, what's He doing throwing the whole world into war, and taking my Dad, and many Dads away—and having the rest of us practice for bombs?

I could only guess we hadn't said the right prayer yet. Or maybe not often enough. One of the big prayers for us regular people—not the priests or nuns—was the rosary. It was the same prayer over and over.

Later in life I was taught all the Hail Mary's in the rosary were mainly sounds or phrases to help put us in a meditative state. And meditative was being quiet inside. This was a huge contradiction to me. Most of the pain in the world, I was beginning to surmise, was because people didn't pay *enough* attention to the words they were saying. Or even worse they didn't *mean* them.

Quiet for me, meditation, silence—could only be with *no* words. Words were and are powerful to me. The other thing that bothered me about the rosary was—all the mysteries I was supposed to contemplate were from somebody else's life. Mostly Mary's, and Jesus', with a little bit of Joseph thrown in.

This was an assault full force, though I never recognized it then, against the possibility that my own life would be fraught with mysteries to contemplate, and sacramental signs to be blessed with, and explore. In fact nobody alive today could be included in the exploration of divine/human connection.

All this came wrapped in a package that included definitive, measurable ways to get and lose God. Assurance at the price of minutiae and their accounting. Not an auspicious foundation for a conversation, even a one-way one. I found myself always looking to clear the field, before I could run in it, or meet anyone there, especially God.

Another part of me, born in my teens, or at least recognized then, began to feel the beauty and ecstasy of communion. With what? Life. Life as it out-pictured on this planet? Life beyond? Beauty itself. Being alive. Being one of the "things" alive. Not being separate from other "things," other beings, alive. The irrepressible onset of this realization, that is recognizing and experiencing something as real *with my whole being*, was a seismic shift for me. Most powerfully a shift into, for the first time, fully trusting *my own* experience in things unseen.

My then-current advisor, a priest, warned me about spiritual pride. I refused to be dampened. I had irrevocably entered the land of "Hide-it-in-his-heart" discovery.

Since then I've opted out of "asking" prayers, as in there might be a God who withholds *anything*. My exceptions are in a foxhole. Till I get my balance.

Who God is has become wonderfully more mysterious—as well as who or what I am. Accepting that I sometimes have a sense of separation from "God," without it ever being possible to be *actually* separate from God, the Divine, the Universe, has also dispelled a lot of the *fear* of the transcendent and my connection or no with it.

I don't think of going outside myself to be in prayer or a prayer state. My mind, my story-self, my ego, my remembered pain body can *only* go outside itself for help. I, the true Self of me, could never go out. Has no need to.

I think of prayer now as a state. *And* an act. The act is to step back from my ego and become aware I am aware of Joe Wise, the story. The state is staying in that place of awareness and openness—in a quiet room, on a walk. In beauty we walk.

I do talk to and ask for help—mostly for understanding and courage, from my dead friends—even those I didn't know—like Gandhi and Elvis. The particular spark of the divine they mirror in me, and I come to see for the first time—or feel I need right now, and can't find. Gandhi for quiet courage and Elvis for gratitude. "Thank you. Thank you very much."

One Self—informing the trees, the stars, and the grass—hidden only slightly in the heart.

★ ★ ★

My favorite sung prayer now is the Native American chant:

> *O Great Spirit*
>
> *Earth, sun, sky, and sea*
>
> *You are inside*
>
> *And all around me.*

Along with perhaps the oldest living prayer chant (in Sanskrit):

> *Om nama Shivaya*
> I bow to, I am connected with, the Divine,
> my true inner Self, the Consciousness that
> dwells in all.

And spoken one:

> *As within, so without.*
>
> *As above, so below.*
>
> *Within, without, and all about.*

Yogananda tells us there is only one prayer we need say: Lord, I yearn
to know Thee.

George Harrison ("My Sweet Lord") might well agree.

Those Among Us

There are those among us

Who are awake

Silent Ones

Everyday Ones

Who carry the Truth

of who we all are

They are the ones

Who daily keep us

from tilting into

chaos and despair

Not unlike the deep sleep

that reconnects us

nightly to our Source

that rights our ship of Sanity.

Christmas '93 - A Winter Solstice

I wasn't afraid of the dark as a kid. Not the outside dark anyway. I had lots of brothers and sisters and an uncle, and I never slept in a room by myself—so I was never physically lonely, or afraid because I was by myself in the dark. I've always *liked* night. I like the quiet and peace of it, though I often disturb it by watching something tense and gripping on video or TV. The night feels more like *my* time and *my* place. I don't give in to others' needs so much then. I'm selfish with the night.

The only time I've experienced pitch black was twice in Mammoth Cave, when the guide doused his light in a large cave room. He had warned us. I was sitting right next to another tourist, and I could feel my leg against hers, and hear other people breathing. I wasn't afraid. If I was by myself, it is likely I would have been—because then there would be no guide, and I would fear getting trapped, maybe lost, and starved.

That's the fear I now know I had as a child on the inside. The dark inside. The void. My emotional life was so strongly discouraged, I learned to douse the lights that would truly guide me into the cave of me. The lights of anger, fear, glad, sad.

Fortunately, there's no time limit on going into the dark. I have found wise men and women who have taken the journey, and who have stood by as I have taken mine. The cave and the dark are ingredients for the birth. The birthing story of Jesus of Nazareth mirrors the truth—laid in a manger in the night in a shallow hillside cave.

The terror of survival (or not) invaded the family early on, thanks to the tetrarch of Galilee, Herod, who was so paranoid about losing power, losing control, he had all the children who *might be* the next king slaughtered. Hitler (slaughtering out of his fear) provided a similar scenario for my family, and my childhood. And when my Dad came back from that war, he found unconscious, artless ways to frighten me out of my "war intimacy" with my Mom, to dethrone me from my "kingship" with her.

I relate in a big way to the shepherds on Christmas night. An angel appears and "the glory of the Lord shone over them." The shepherds were frightened. The angel says, No need to be—I have good news for you. I know what it's like to my bones, to stand in great light, and hear good news, and still be scared. Part of my fear is, I haven't earned this, so how can it be true and real? I haven't made it or caused it. I can't control it, and I can't control its withdrawal. To be more confident with my inner life, I often choose to live in some darkness, or hold on to some tension. They are familiar.

Lately, in Quaker rooms especially, though I know it can be anywhere I can get still, the darkness within rolls away, or dissipates. I move beyond the poles of opposites, and light-and-dark (much as to a blind person I suppose) is a non-issue. Being able to get still is a sometimes thing—but that I can at all, I attribute at least partly, to my past willingness to follow the star into the cave. The light within guiding me to face the implanted fears, the self-perpetuated fears, the anger, the hurt, the grief. To bring them out of the cave. Epiphany them and me, and be welcomed by friends who were safe to trust this dimension of me with. Others who have followed that star.

This year we've put a sun on top of the tree and omitted the creche. The angel that flew at the top of the tree for years is still in the room and much closer on a low, hollied table. No creche, to me, says I honor the light within Jesus of Nazareth, *and* I honor the light within Sophie of Dayton, the newest-on-earth soul of my blood family.

Jesus' blood family is listed back to Abraham in Matthew's account of his birth. It is mostly men who are chronicled. Some women make

Joe Wise

it in parentheses. One I know from long-ago studies was a prostitute. I like not omitting her.

I have just discovered, and it is good news of great joy to me, that my lineage includes, four generations back, a woman of the Cherokee nation. So far I know only that she was called "Miss Sallie" (I hope to find her tribal name), and that she wore a mantle, that had beaded into it a cornucopia of medicinal herbs and roots and spices. A healer. A priestess. My family could use one. Couldn't we all? I will follow after the star of her person, in whatever courthouses and conversations I will find need for, after the holidays.

Meanwhile, the sun we placed on top of the tree, especially at night, reminds me of the cycle of things. In the year cycle, this is the night of the shortest day. In four days, Christmas day, the Naval observatory, counting days in minutes, will confirm that the light *is* one minute longer with us and increasing.

It is so much easier to believe death is forever in the Fall, than to believe life is forever in the Spring. It is so much easier to believe life is good in the long day, than in the long night. Day. Light. Sun. It will come 'round again out of this darkness. *We* will come 'round again out of our darkness. *And* we will come 'round again to the moon and into the darkness. "And so it continued both day and night." Noel.

A Winter's Tale

It was a regular morning. That, of course, has taken on new meaning here in my 70th year, and some time before, but that's not where I'm going. I'm going to the track to run my 5 miles—as I do every other day. Not every other day, as in I run every day, but as in run one, skip one. This is taking me as long to get into my "story" as it does to get ready to run.

I began running cross country for my Boy Scout troop when I was 12. With rare pauses for injuries, I've been on this path, this runner's path ever since. It is one of the most prized gifts of my life. For most of that time I've bounded out of bed, slipped into my shoes, and I'm out the door. Now I'm more like a butterfly. Not light-on-my-feet butterfly, but stages of butterfly—caterpillar, larva. Like that. It involves Johnson and Johnson, Dr. Scholl's and Ben Gay, along with a cocoon's age worth of stretching. I may be over-doing the stretching thing from what I read lately—but anything I even remotely believe keeps me flexible at my age, physically or psychologically—I will do and do and do.

The track here at Mingus Union High School is low tech. Translation: packed high desert dirt with infrequent over-sanding. Arizona's answer to a cinder track. It works for me. I also run some of the trails here around Sedona. Not as often any more, since it's a gamble on footing, and therefore injury. All my paths now are soft. Haven't been on roads or pavement for decades. If my knees and joints could write, I know I'd get a Christmas card, and maybe even a Valentine from them, every year.

We've started, Maleita (my wife) and I, a Christmas tradition with Bob here. Bob is part of the "regular" of regular morning. He is the field manager at Mingus. Tends it, feeds it, plants it, nurtures it, lines it. It's actually *fields* for him. Several, including a baseball diamond. But this is the one *I* see him at most, the football/soccer one, on the inside of the track. With ever-shrinking budget, he fights the good fight, to keep it green and strong and ready, for the physical exuberance and mayhem of teen athletes.

His regular gear at this time of year includes a Green Bay hoodie. From Wisconsin. Still has family there. He's as faithful to his Favre-less Packers as he is to his fields. Not unlike a quarterback, he barks signals now and then to his field crew, especially loud when motorized equipment is in the picture. This morning is quiet, and there's lots of banter involving various NFL franchises, players, and playoff possibilities.

The "tradition" we've started with Bob, this is year number 2, is to give him the annual *Farmer's Almanac*. Having been a janitor and groundskeeper at a school in my late teens and early twenties, I have some sense of the demands, and neverendingness, and urgent requests that come with this service. And the relatively low level of expressions of appreciation. We hope our almanac lifts the level. It will also give him another connection with his silent partners in the fields: the weather, and the weather Maker.

Another regular is *not* here *this* morning. Probably came earlier. Ghost, and his partner Cayle. Ghost is canine. Cayle is human. Ghost, I would venture to say, is the finest athlete ever to take the field at Mingus. He is a streak, a blur, a white flash, a joy. He is a Porsche to my Vespa. I haven't asked, but I bet Cayle named him so, because you keep asking yourself "where did he go?" "He was just here." Not having lived on the savannas in Africa, I have personally not seen another being on the planet run with such grace, efficiency, and abandon. Another gift under my year-round "tree of life," as well as this year's Christmas one.

At the far end of the track on a feeder road, sits an "intermittent" regular. A fire truck and an accompanying ambulance. They beat us here this time. The crews are already out, and stretching and jogging, and running up and down the stands. A periodic piece of their fitness program. Every time I see them here, I tell myself there would never be a better time or place to have an I'm-coming-home-Elizabeth heart event. Yes, I'm Sanford and Son old. While my admiration for all the daring they do goes on unabated, my gratitude for their fidelity to this "hidden" part of their readiness, surges with each of their appearances here.

Another not-here-regular is Dennis. Also an early bird. Likely come and gone. We share retirement from teaching, and body wisdom, carefully harvested from years of repair, tune ups, and general maintenance. We're hoping we hold up like Hondas. 300,000 miles would be nice.

Everything feels in place. People, patterns, predictable. My gloves and my headband. Heartbeat and breath. Regular. Regular. Crash. How could I not have seen them coming? The "crash" is a big bass drum and cymbal. One piece of *the* irregular element of this morning, trackside: a marching band (all terms used loosely except "a"). Nine barely-teen trainees, each already proving they can march to the beat of a different...let's just say Thoreau would be proud. Some are risking momentary herniation.

We had awakened this morning, one of us, with John Denver's "Today is the First Day (of the Rest of my Life)" wafting through our subconscious. Whoever it was hummed a little, and it engaged both of us, pleasantly, meditatively, inside and sometimes out, till this very moment. The band, is suddenly blowing and striking in various pitches and cadences, "Jingle Bell Rock." As I run past (the walking) Maleita, I say, "Oh well, there goes John Denver." "Jingle Bell Rock" trumps about anything but "It's a Small World" and "Rocky Top." Next lap she says, "This whole thing reminds me of Charlie Brown's Christmas." I throw back over my shoulder: "The band IS the tree."

I find myself smiling, to no one. I am reminded that I am not Pavo Nurmi or Lasse Viren, no flying Finn, yet here I am. That music, is so wonderfully democratic and without price, in its origin and its destination. That the Spirit of Christmas can break out anywhere. It carries me forward. It carries *us* forward.

On trumpet, on tuba

On Green Bay and ground crew

On fireman, on medic

On Dennis and Ghost too

On your marks

On your marks

You runners all

Now dash away

Dash away

Dash away all.

The Meaning of Christmas

December, we call it. A cold dark period that could only be rescued by a baby. One who reminds us of the gift of life and its eternal persistence. One who reminds us there is no opposite of life. (Death is the opposite of *birth*.) Life *is*. As God, Source, *is*. And this particular baby grew to know and teach this as few ever have. Paying particular attention to deflecting exclusiveness, or even specialness. Being of God is a given. Realizing it, while in this body, this December body, is an act of heroic surrender. Heroic, even as we see how foolhardy it is to believe anything else. To act as if anything else were true. It's the kind of surrender only a child could allow. A child of God. As all are.

Happy birthday, Jesus. The child in you carried the day.

My turn.

Thank you.

I Get So Anxious

I get so anxious

on the in-betweens.

Between events,

experiences, actions,

programs, paintings,

writings.

Gaps in a schedule,

unexpected delays.

I feel like I'm

losing

valuable time,

growth, opportunities,

my role as a contributor,

who I am, even.

No wonder stillness

is such a hard path.

Silence

Another one-word launch in journal group.

Silence is golden. It can't be silver—we ring silver bells; or brass—we blow *it* in pitches; or steel—we beat it as tone drum. This expression must have been born before platinum. When gold was the most precious. Silence, the most precious thing on earth. Makes complete sense.

Yet here I am doing my part—on my outside—*and* my inside to make some noise, albeit most in harmony, or pleasing. On the inside a near constant chatter, mostly reminding myself what I'm currently doing, and slipping in periodic "heads ups" on what I'm doing next.

When I'm least conscious of squandering my silence, is when I'm asking the "what" and "why" questions. What keeps in balance the stars in the sky? Why do we war? Most of the time though is not on the question, but on my unique and highly-beneficial-to-the-world-sure-fire solutions, answers, and directions to go.

There is nothing more peaceful than silence. Yet I consistently oust it for my mental gnawing, usually on my largest bone.

I know nothing in me produces more fear, than feeling out of control. My mind accommodates my discomfort by relentless reasoning, searching, composting, and harvesting what comes after question marks.

Yet another great contemporary seer, Eckhart Tolle, points out to us our mind, and its activity—while enjoying its role as our finest and funnest tool—also likes to actually take over, and become All of the all of me.

I wonder if, age after age, we think we are the most challenged to live on the planet, and still know peace, especially the peace of silence.

For Henry David Thoreau it was rough—and only the woods and pond would do. H. W. L. Poonja, the Indian mystic known as Papaji, was constantly taking his students out of the meditation room, and into the marketplace, to practice stillness on the move. Silence in the noise.

These guys might well throw up their hands, and their lunches, if they could see our ipods, cellphones, blackberries, smart pads, and beyond. We might all celebrate the Bose headphones—not for sound—though they can well be used that way. But the new ones for silence. Without our intermediate weapon—white noise. Or blocking sound with more subtle sound. Bose says—hey we're just knocking it all back.

That's it. That's what I need. A Bose brain. There's got to be an allele in our DNA we could mutate.

Yet here we are—choosing to be out of the silence we came from—deliberately choosing, or accepting the invitation, to be immersed in the cacophony and symphony of human life. Deathly screams and Italian tenors. Hunger cries and satisfied "goos." Sifting and sorting our way, through the precious and not-so-precious metals of our lives—feeling balance mostly, if not only, in the gold.

Unlikely

From this vantage point

and this vintage point

in my life

it seems highly unlikely

anything but this is true:

You can't grow

and look good

at the same time.

Uncertainty

remains

the most fertile

egg

Trees

In the winter of '89 I was asked to write a song for a tree-planting ceremony. Anchorage, Kentucky, one of many communities to carry the moniker "Tree City USA," would host this event in the Spring. G. H. W. Bush, the current President of the United States, would attend and be the ceremonial planter. Anchorage lies at the outer fringe of Louisville, my then home, a city replete with public ("saved nature") parks and uncounted legions of trees therein. The President was coming. We Louisvillians had been blessed by the presence, foresight, and Gaian design skills of Frederick Olmstead, who set aside acre after acre of park land in almost two dozen locations, all named for a Native American tribe. I grew up closest to Algonquin and Shawnee parks. Mr. Olmstead, of course,was the St. Francis of New York, saving that city from complete concrete flooring and unchecked urban glut, with Central Park. In a recent Life section of *USA Today*, recommending the ten best places in America "to see trees this spring," Louisville was first on the list, with Olmstead's eighteen parks as the capstone. The President was coming. I had written and recorded hundreds of songs. None of them with a deadline. None of them *with*, no *for*, no—*to be sung at a ceremony with*, the President of the United States. And secret service men.

I set about the task, the process of composing. It was not going well. Part of the deadline included some lead time to teach the song to the students at Anchorage Middle School. I love trees. I am juiced about trees. I am dry about the song. I was already going to my last mental ploy, which is this will be *a* song, not *the* song. The President was coming. It wasn't working. And as with many major events in my life, most of them interior, I found flow only on and in surrender. One morning in my run at Seneca Park, my closest tribe as an adult, I stopped before my favorite ancient Oak, embraced it, and asked it out loud to help me sing its praises. After breakfast the song tumbled out of me, almost all of it in a single sitting.

Plant me a tree

Watch it grow

Feed it with love

Talk to its soul

Let it grow free

Plant me a tree

Set it right down

Into the ground

Where its true mother

Can be found

Let it go free

Plant me a tree.

The chorus. With melody. I thanked "my" Oak silently, and did so in person the next day.

This is for you

This is for me

This is for earth and wind

  and sky and bright rolling sea

For sister bird

For brother squirrel

This is for every creature

  great and small in this world.

The verses came out, affirming my place, the tree's place, in the family of things.

I gave a home-recorded cassette of the piece to the school's music director. I didn't hear from her. Was it too hard, melodically? Worse, was it too weird an approach? We were scheduled for one rehearsal with the kids. My friend and guitarist buddy, Dennis, was joining me. Dan, a new friend, was engineering. Two guitars, a lead vocal and the kids comprised the channels.

I walked into the packed auditorium. Some kids were on stage. The rest in the seats. I say a quick hi to the music teacher/director, and do not get a single clue from her face whether she thinks we are about to launch the Titanic here, or NASA's newest.

From the first chord we went into orbit. The first time I look up from my sheet music, I see row after row after row of little singers at full throat moving together in cascading gestures. It is a stunning sight. The director had choreographed the song. It made it like a kite with good wind. When we finished rehearsal, I was ready for the President. And the cameras. It would be professionally video-taped by Ron, a recent collaborator, as well as captured live by news people.

President Bush didn't come. At the last minute he decided to plant a tree in Indianapolis instead. It was in honor of Ryan White, the high schooler who had before, with his recent death, changed the face of Aids. I liked the choice for many reasons. Mostly for the public sign of beginning to address this disease, and to do so with compassion. It also gave me, and all of us at Anchorage on Arbor Day, a chance to focus on the tree, and the planting, and not so much on the planter.

Oh I thank you for your skeletons on Winter's sky

I thank you for your greening ways in Spring

I thank you for the shade and shadows late in June

For the hymn in Fall your blazing branches sing.

We were outdoors. Among the trees. Singing and gesturing. Planting. It was simple. It was moving. It was full. I couldn't wait to tell my Oak.

★　★　★

The recording of this song at this event, "Plant Me a Tree," is available on itunes, at www.giamusic.com, and amazon.com, as a single or on the collection The Best of Joe Wise... Music for Kids, Volume 2. The complete lyric is in the piece following.

Plant Me a Tree

Chorus:

Plant me a tree

Watch it grow

Feed it with love

Talk to its soul

Let it grow free

Plant me a tree

Set it right down

Into the ground

Where its true mother

Can be found

Let it go free

Plant me a tree.

Verse 1:

This is for you

This is for me

This is for earth and wind

    and sky and bright rolling sea

For sister bird

For brother squirrel

This is for every creature

    great and small in this world.

Verse 2:

I thank you for the song you sing in my guitar

I thank you for the roof that covers my head

I thank you for the ships that sail the open sea

And for the rest I find upon my bed.

Verse 3:

Oh I thank you for your skeletons on winters' sky

I thank you for your greening ways in spring

I thank you for the shade and shadows late in June

Joe Wise

For the hymn in fall your blazing branches sing.

Verse 4:

    I'm in the tree

    The tree is in me

    We feel the life of life

       in veins and limbs flowing free

    We stretch out our arms

    We welcome our friends

    Each day the loving circle grows

       the dance has no end.

★ ★ ★

The recording of this song, "Plant Me a Tree," is available on itunes, at www.giamusic.com and amazon.com as a single or on the collection The Best of Joe Wise...Music for Kids,Vol. 2

Alicia, by Phone

I talked to Alicia yesterday. She's my only grandchild. She's in Denver. She's 7. She's my "yuv." More about *that* ("yuv ") later.

I am so 833 miles *not* from Denver. But Ma Bell, or some iteration of her, is—and puts her Colorado voice in my Arizona ear.

This time it's about all things Harry Potter. She's in the middle of book 3, *The Prisoner of Azkaban* and reads one chapter a night, seeing each *movie* only at the completion of the book. I've given up being startled at her levels of vocabulary and comprehension. For a long distance grandfather it's a gift beyond measure. She seemed to spill right out of the womb reader-ready. And fiction–ready. Some, her own. These may start during a rare cherished visit or they may start wirelessly. Some play well in both arenas.

One of her earliest was in her room, involved some cardboard crowns, fairly elaborate self costuming and some upcoming royal nuptials. Long before there was Will and Kate there was Alicia and Prince Papa. Maleita was told she would have minimal involvement in the ceremony and practically nothing at the reception, but she could come. Alicia then remembered she needed a minister, so Gran moved up to a speaking part. But a rather meager portion of wedding cake was all she got at the reception. After the vows and Gran's fabulous ad lib, Alicia turns to me and says (during a time her initial letter l's were mysteriously letter y's): "Come, my yuv. We'll kiss and dance. Then ride away."

By the third pass at all this, just when I was showing some advanced competency in my royal role, we moved on. Fate is fickle.

Next we were all cast as good baker, bad baker, and customer. I ask what makes a bad baker. Like he *burns* the muffins? No. It turns out he doesn't use the time-honored ingredients of accepted confectionery practice but rather small creatures, mostly from the insect kingdom and various types of soil, moist *or* dry. This quickly degenerates, or ascends, depending on your point of view, into a gross-out contest. We break for the evening. I relax into the supper of her good-baker mother, Michelle.

This particular scenario, good baker/ bad baker, was the first Alicia carried over to phone visits. It lent itself well, especially in the audio production department. Knocks. Doorbells. Opening and closing doors were introduced. We shuffled characters and then others would appear, calling for dual roles. Each bakery event was quite unique and began often to spin into malfeasance of some order, poisonings, kidnappings, thus necessitating the birth of Sgt.Daigle (Alicia's last name), who was the go-to guy in all out-of-control, heavily mayhem-saturated eventualities. We could then add vocal sirens too. Mine was always the best.

Among the scenes she set and characters she cast when we were live, that is, with her physically—one of my favorites was the library. We never shifted roles there. *She* was *always* the librarian. Gran and I were always parents from two different families. Alicia begins by setting up her considerable collection plus actual library books she currently has out, all atop a long divider shelf in the room.

"Now, how old is your child?" she asks me.

"Six." I respond.

"Boy or girl?"

"Boy."

"And what does he like?"

"Well, he likes his stuffed animals."

"I've got just the book for him. Take this Winnie the Pooh one. It's a sweet story."

I'm thinking, they *all* have honey in them, but I don't ask for clarification because Gran has already been tapped to profile her little girl. I thumb through my book and the librarian takes on an unexpected sternness. "No, you can't look at your books till you get home." It remains the one lapse in my laser focus on the "star" in our 7-year history.

Alicia, the librarian, was herself a good storyteller from very young. The first I remember was the day after Gran and I took her for a ride on Denver's light rail from Englewood to downtown and back. In the middle of a procession of dry Cheerios to her mouth she paused, stared off and said, " 'Member, train go fast Papa hold you?" I did. I do.

I also remember holding her day-old, fresh skin-wrapped self over my shoulder, humming " Hobo's Lullaby," reminding me more than *her* how temporary *all* homes are, the physical ones, the planetary ones—and affirming to *both* of us the everlastingness of the heart ones.

A little like the photo I now keep pinned on the cork board in front of my desk—of Alicia, holding me. She is still pre-verbal and her face takes up most of the image. I have lain her on the bed and bent over her. All you can see of me is a lot of forehead and a little hair (thus the temporary theme). What there is of it she is grasping and pulling at with unrestrained glee, and the photo catches her in a pause, a sideways glance with the hint of a tongue in the corner of her mouth, all the while maintaining a till–death–do–us–part grip on the hair—and me. Everlasting.

These are the connections that lead you to beyond-your-means-cookie-dough-over-the-phone purchases. Even if the school is flush, which of course, it isn't. It's a school. *And* they lucked into her.

We saw some of the foreshadowings of her marketing savvy years ago, when she came to our motel in Denver and started selling us things we brought along. Play money. But, hey. It culminated in selling us ice in refilled trays from the room frig. Refilled with water. In the bathroom. When I complained that it wasn't ice, I was instructed to take it home and put it in my home frig, and that'll be $6.46. In this case the Iceman *goeth*. To his own freezer.

I *am* at home, *talking* to her of many things. It's funny how we use the phrase talking to somebody when we speak of phone conversations. The truth is I was mostly *listening* to her, about many things. Talking *with* would get it.

I was *getting* a series of giant rolling waves of enthusiasm crashing on the shore of my ready heart. Soccer was the current tide. She was getting on a team. Wearing real soccer shoes. She would have a number. She so had mine.

Back again to Harry Potter. And muggles. And Hogwarts. And before I was aware, she had morphed into an entrepreneur/telemarketer and I am hearing: "So, Mr. Wise, would you like to order all the *ten* magic wands—including Harry's and Hermoine's—and have the eleventh one be free?" And, "We are offering two models of vehicles for Quidditch (which I note to myself is like air soccer on brooms)—we have the Nimbus 2000 model or the Fire-bolt." Back in business.

At a time in my life, in my 70's, when I now and again wonder if I'll become irrelevant—in many ways, but especially to her, I pull back a time she was a teacher and I was her student and she kept giving me harder and harder things to do. I raised my hand and said, "Teacher, I don't know if I can do all of this." She walked up to seated me with her teacher apron on, took my face between her two little hands, looked right into my eyes, and said, "You don't have to worry, Papa, you are my rocker star." I melted.

Meanwhile, I buy a boatload of everything Harry Potter, hang up and hope I live to be 90. So I can hop aboard my Nimbus 2000, crank up my Draco Malfoy magic wand and go visit my "yuv."

Rafsanjani. *Et Cum Spiritu Tuo*

A journal group piece. We all blindly chose two images. Used both. I drew a picture of a man sculpting a human form in a church, with stained glass windows, and one of a man reading at a desk in a library. I had just heard, again, the name Rafsanjani on last night's news and saw the Catholic liturgy changes on morning news at CNN.

Rafsanjani. *Et cum spiritu tuo.* I've always loved the name Rafsanjani. From the first moment I heard it. I associate it with the Mid East. Islam. I totally love the sound of it. Rafsanjani. Does it mean ""Raef-Son of Johnny?" Or as we in the West would say it, "Raef Johnson" or "Ralph Johnson (John's son)?" It *may* mean "death to all infidels"—of which I would be one. I hope it doesn't.

The meaning we assign to sounds is so arbitrary. But once assigned, can become deathless, or in this case may be death*full*. The time, effort, and gift of seeking out *another's* meaning—that is, our lack of same—is basically what's keeping the world from peace. Fear of the possible difference. Difference equals unsureness, and insecurity. In an insecure world, rife with haves and have-nots, we become so fearful, we get mad to cover the fear, and begin our relentless "My Imam is better than yours "…"My Pope knows more than your Ayatollah." Security can only come from someone being absolutely "right." And then when the absolutely "wrongs" can't admit it, they've got to be obliterated, removed from the equation.

The messes of the world are all God's doing, because *we* haven't done the "right" things yet. The infidels haven't been erased.

Et cum spirit tuo. A top story on CNN. Catholics changing their Mass responses. *Dominus vobiscum,* already grammatically ambiguous, has been translated as "The Lord *be* with you." Like there's no way he could already actually be there with you. The alternate translation is "The Lord *is* with you." Nope. "And with your spirit," the new response to the old Latin. Not, "And also with you." Presumably because God could never be with our bodies. They were a mistake from the beginning and the sooner we get rid of them, the better. "The Lord is with you," "And also with you" smacks strongly of *Namaste*—"I honor the Divine in you"—and who knows that that wouldn't lead to Rafsanjani, and we're off to the infidel races.

I know this pattern in myself. I get afraid. I get mad. I close down.

I now have empathy. I am grateful for my awareness, and for having compassion for me in my process. My anger now is not so much about "I have to be right to feel secure"—but about the sleep so many of the world's leaders and "teachers" can't seem to wake up from.

We are the ones assigning meaning to places and languages and teachings. Like the sculptor fashioning himself, in the light of a stained glass window and its picturings. Like the scholar and historian, who reads only the books that "his" people have written— thinkers aligned with him. History of the victors—the *only* writers of history.

I wish I had a magic want to wave over all the Ralph Johnsons and Rafsanjanis of the world. A day where the only words spoken were "the Lord is with you"—and the only response—"*Namaste.*"

Most Wanted

What if we are wanting the wrong people?

What if *America's Most Wanted* was Eckhart Tolle?

or the Dalai Lama,

Deepak Chopra,

or me,

fully aware?

Annie

Annie is open for viewing today. The newest Patron Saint of Humor. With her, you could easily escalate to bladder-conscious silly. She probably won't be "precious"—one of the many categories she sought to achieve, depending on the significance of the event. I don't remember them all, but I believe they started with "cute" and zenithed out at "precious," with "adorable" as its penultimate. Earrings, makeup, coiffure were some of the elements in the equations, by dint of inclusion or sophistication. "Precious" is precluded this time, because her soul and spirit are "not there." Someone at the funeral home did the ministrations.

This, in some reverse kind of way, is a gift and a plus to me, in my not being there, in Louisville. In Arizona she is "precious." My picturing has let Annie do the cosmetics. My picturing of her true Self, now not encapsulated by a body struggling for air, is beyond the limits of categories. Free, at last. From all the concerns *about* appearances, available to all the capacities *for* appearances. Maleita is already asking for, and receiving these. At the track yesterday morning, a brand new synthetic one, with brand new fencing, she was communing with Annie and saying, "Show me the funny." Not really. More like, "Show me we can still make contact." She looked up, with the tilt of her water bottle, to a new sign saying, "Any questions or comments, *call* us…" Maleita didn't spit out her water. She could've. It *was* funny. It was both. It was Annie.

Annie had teased Maleita about talking to her dead friends. Maleita had already sat on the couch, after the phone call that Annie had passed, and said, "Ok, Annie, this is my transmission number one." We're taking the "Call us" as Annie's first.

She, Annie, had already had an appearance not long ago in *her* life. As she sat by her dying Father's bedside overnight, the morning brought his getting up, leaving his breakfast, telling her goodbye, putting on his fedora, and waving. Just then, the nurse woke her, and said, "Your father is passing."

While I remind myself in my grief, to be grateful for all her appearances in my life, and Maleita's, over the last 50 years, I open myself to the possibility of timeless appearances. On *this* side of the veil. And the other. I see me greeting her now.

I see me greeting her then, "Hi, Annie, you precious one…"

Hide and Seek

Written in journal group. Topic: favorite game from childhood, and why.

The world's greatest game. Most popular. Most long lasting. From peek-a-boo, to psychotherapy, to meeting death. We love a mystery. I love to disappear now and again, yet never be lost. I love to be the seeker, who is safe enough, for a friend to re-appear again—to themselves, to me.

I love to play detective, if only in my mind, and ferret out some hidden truth. Court TV, it's spinoffs, and Harlan Coben feed this need. At least it *seems* a need.

I love to surprise people. Keep something hidden till just the right moment. The punch line in a funny story. Constructing a path on the way that makes the punch come from the most unexpected hiding place.

I love to surprise people with what I can do, or have done. Especially if we meet in the neutral-est of circumstances. "Oh, yes, I swam the Atlantic." This love for pulling something big out of hiding leads us down some tricky roads. Our need, I guess, to be more and more spectacular, so we'll be valued more and more.

It's funny, but the people I'm most drawn to, are people who come out of hiding right away. "Oh yeah, I could drown with a spoon full of water." Or sometimes I'm drawn into the "swam the Atlantic" person, to see if I can detect anything else in their story that says—"well, I swam on the cruise ship while we crossed the Atlantic." Reel them back into the level of normalcy I live in.

Watching my grandchild Alicia, now 3, when she was truly little, play peek-a-boo, reminded me of how delightful a truth it is, that we all can come and go, and come and go, without losing each other.

Court TV's Masterminds tells story after story of a thief who takes things for years—hiding not only what he steals through elaborate fencings, but his own identity, and both sometimes for decades. While I'm drawn to these for the hide and seek content, I luckily find no allure in taking what is not mine. The psychic/moral pain of that remains a welcome deterrent.

I sometimes see my whole big-picture-trip on earth, as having its basis in hide and seek. I am a spark of the Divine. A flash of the eternal. Choosing to cover this over with the mud of earth and human life—as part of the requirement for the trip. For the experience.

When somebody obviously breaks through the hiding-human curtain like the Dalai Lama, or the checker who helps the old man to his car, I go, "Aha! I found you." And in this I find me. And in the quiet.

My trip down therapy lane—during which I truly did swim the Atlantic, my own story became clear enough to *be* a story, and not me. "Aha."

I ask myself to trust this lifelong game, and it's always surprising, yet ever-constant outcome, when I arrive at the doors of death. I will find *me* there. Me, never separated from the Divine. Aha. Help my unbelief. Maybe that's my bottom line treasure from all my experiences—and why I, not quite ready, am still alive on *this* plane. Yeah, I've still got some peek-a-boos left in me. Bet you don't know where it is: Where *I* am? *Who* I am?

Me Party

I'm thinking

the best and truest

picture of me

exists as a sauna

with all my selves

present, naked,

and accounted for.

A party.

The heat to bring it.

Me to own it.

All.

The Meaning of Life

A writing from journal group. This invitation: "You are attending a lecture at Northern Arizona University. The scheduled speaker is the Dalai Lama. The student body is primed. The Dalai Lama is suddenly not feeling well. The university president seeks you out in the assembly, taps you on the shoulder, and asks you to step in for His Holiness. His topic, now yours, is 'The Meaning of Life.'"

"The Meaning of Life"—a big topic. But it didn't scare Monty Python off, so I won't run from it either.

The meaning of life, in college, for me—who is the only one I can vouch for—and even that with infrequent certitude—was please the people around me enough to go on with things I liked. I liked being away from home—but not completely on my own. The beginning of self-autonomy without having to do much beyond my laundry. I figured studying and getting pretty good grades, would keep my family and the faculty happy with me staying there.

I loved the possibilities part of those years. Mine and the world's. I majored in philosophy, so there was much possibility and a smorgasbord of meaning. This was the main thing I learned in college. *My* views about meaning on the broad scale, were one set among many. Only long after college did I learn that meaning for *me*, on the scale of *my* life, was entirely up to me. In fact I have come to equate that admission, and acting upon it, as the single most defining characteristic of maturity. Taking charge of my own life.

I am reminded of a response by an artist friend of mine, when a viewer once asked him what a particularly nebulous (representation-wise) sculpture meant. He said simply: "That's not my job."

So I tell myself—sometimes the way I sculpt and live my life, will have apparent, and pleasing interpretations, by myself and by those around me. At other times, I or we, may not have a clue. The part of myself that craves meaning, goes lost and loony during these times, and begins to find similar outpicturings in the lives of those around me, and I begin frequently to say things like—"Oh, it all has meaning—it's just not clear yet." "The universe is friendly." "You're gonna be so much stronger." I now classify this as whistling-in-the-dark 101, and preaching-what I-need-to-hear-and-want-to-believe 501. I have become open to the belief that some things just happen. Chaos theory—which of course is way less threatening than "chaos." Put a "theory" with anything and the illusion of a harness or cage appears. Chaos happens. Random events. Nothing personal. You're in the game, so the ball and other players are free agents and unpredictable sometimes. Sometimes they all collide with you, instead of going into formation with you.

And those who tell me, "Oh, you're gonna be stronger" I want to just crown. I want to tell them, "One day we'll look back on all this and—throw up."

But what does it all mean? Part of me feels more comfortable when I can "say" or "predict." Another part when I *can* or *do*, feels profoundly bored. The deepest part of me knows I'm in a mystery. And I love a mystery. I love peek-a-boo. The game. The mystery. Now you see me. Now you don't. Now *I* see me. Now I don't. Now I see what it all means. Now I don't.

I *have* come to believe, that in the graduate school of my life, I am my own homeroom, at the end of the day. My own *home*, at the end of the day. All these experiences and questions have arisen and disappeared. I remain. Remain with yourself. You can't help it anyway. Love yourself, and each other, more than any meaning.

And don't forget recess.

Regina and the Shopper

My friend Regina did a thesis, PhD.wise, that explored near-death experiences in a time most thought it too woo woo.

Besides the model of her courage, she also brought forth this story of a lady who, when she was in the "beyond" before the "back," had a Presence lead her back to a scene in her life where, on an ordinary day, she walked out of a store onto the vast paved world in front of it, and on the way to her car saw one determined flower finding its way up and through the black. And she put down her bag, and knelt, and kissed it with her eyes.

The Presence (Angel?) then told her that her action here was of profound import for the ongoing growth, harmony, and evolution of the world.

This was the entirety of her "life review."

Adhesive Tape

This piece was born in journal group. We were presented a brown paper bag filled with household items. Pick two without peeking. Choose one. Write.

I'm stuck with this. No, I choose it. I celebrate its existence. Along with the molefoam from Dr. Scholl's I cut out to accommodate the calluses on my sole, it helps me continue to run 5 miles comfortably. It is a reminder I am older. I ran for years without it. It is also a miracle run-saver. Most things in my life are both. It is an everyday reminder that, by many standards, I am flawed, defective, imperfect, short of the ideal. I move my intention toward it not being *my* standard. It is a reminder to take myself as I am, today, into account. More than the economy is sagging. The beard dye I use is called "the rejuvenator." Can Viagra and Rogaine be far behind? I'm blissfully free of wheelchair and crutch, *and* my left ankle hurts when I'm on it too long. Most of my 63 years have been ankle-worry-free, oblivious even. Much of my new attention to my body comes, when the life cycle rolls around to getting me more fully into my own life. Kids raised, spouse on a roll, many friends sick and transitioning.

Waterproof—something that would stand up in the ocean maybe—but I settle for it being impervious to my own sweat for the duration of a 50-minute run. I stop each time I ready myself to run, to tape my foot. It is a great and new, counting-all-the-years sign to me, that I take care of my body. It is comforting to see me this much on my own side, and not sacrificing my body for my or somebody else's current perceived want or need.

I like bandaids and sports tape for what they address. I've been active. I've been engaged. Fully. I carry a scar or a burr or a tear as my badge of participation, maybe even excellence. It's my war ribbon for the current campaign. A thing possibly admired. I don't have to tell people I walked into a door. They can assume a risky adventure, or even a harrowing rescue.

I remember a love-hate relationship with iodine as a kid—hated the burn—loved the badge of stain. I liked dried blood and scabbing the best. It reminded me I could survive knocks and scuffs and falls and bruises—most were not fatal. I could engage myself more fully in the physical universe. Skates were worth the scrapes.

There was something tender and communion-like and age-erasing, to have a grownup bandage me as a kid—treat my wound. A leveler. I loved it when they would say, "this is going to burn"—or "hurt." I didn't trust anybody who said, "this won't hurt a bit"—not just about the iodine—but about life.

I like when someone can attend to me, and not have *their* wounds be the story, or more "important" than mine. Maybe I just don't like to have pain competes. Sharing for communion—yes.

Tape—binding the wounds—covering the hurts—letting old feet run—what a great invention. My time here is up, and that just about wraps it up.

Maybe This

No one would ever

mistake him for George Clooney.

Ruddy faced

rough handed

squat framed

seeker at Walmart

with his weathered white tee

and Budweisered cap.

Already casting his lot

in this ocean of choices

and making his way

to checkout

with a cellophane cone

of cut flowers

and a small red bear.

His gait was not graceful

but short, tenta–tentative

steps, en route it seems,

to meet

some unseen executioner,

with eyes

both lost and afraid.

February 14th

had never

looked so brutal.

And so brave.

Joe Wise

Charlotte Ann, Letter to
Another Favorite Teacher

Dear Sr. Charlotte Ann,

This will be a love letter. You embodied that so beautifully for me—Love—I could never have used that word then. Lucky for me you spilled over onto both sides of my seventh grade. You stayed the same toward me, whether you were my teacher or not.

I loved how you treated me, looked at me, were present to me—direct, frowning, smiling, questioning, admiring. I loved the gift of the transparency of your face—and trusting your current self to you. And to me.

I loved sitting with you on the steps where you lived. None of the other nuns did this. I loved the long silences—I had only experienced silence with somebody or bodies else at supper, when my Dad would, as randomly as getting the wrong spoon for his coffee, impose it. Silence with you was a comfort, and just as easy as talking.

It was in our quiet I first heard the actual sound of a diving bird's wings as he braked and torqued himself for the pullout. I am grateful you could show me I didn't have to speak, and describe everything.

You were so vulnerable in the schoolyard games—basketball, volleyball, dodgeball—handicapped by the habit—*and* refusing to let it be a dictator.

You were able to teach me of growth and caring and the soul's life, without all the trappings of shame and guilt that seemed to drown out all else in the hierarchic church we lived in. With you, Jesus never died for my sins. He just had a chance to be like you.

I thank you for all the courage and self-belief and work you did to get so comfortable in your own skin, to trust yourself to the moment. To take yourself seriously *and* hilariously. I loved your laugh. It was almost always at some new blip on your own screen. It gave me and all of us so much permission. I am still reaping the rewards of it.

I always loved being consoled by you. You had a way of doing that that made me feel taller and fuller rather than diminished by *your* current wellbeing. I liked it so much, I made up a couple of things. I can see your smile as you read this last sentence.

You would have been a shining star for me at any age—but in the U. S. A. in the 1940's and 50's, in the Roman Catholic Church of the same era, you were Amelia Earhart, and I thank you for blessing *my* wings.

Love,

Joe

Running the Track by the Mingus Mountains

I lift up my eyes

to the mountains.

I feel in me

the strength, the heavy

of the mighty Mingus

rock,

the comfort, the ease

of the billowy pillowy

clouds

nestling all about.

I love the

bothness in me.

Hearts and Guardians

My friend Sandy has brought the practice of Soulcollage Cards[12] to our geography. Maleita brought this image home from a session. Sandy assembled it. It is of a woman cradling a/her heart in great reverence and cosmic light. Below her is a fierce phalanx of nine Doberman's standing at-the-ready in front of a golden luxury car. Conjoining the two images is a plastic replica of a human heart with appropriate aortic "arms." This heart is wrapped in chains.

Be still my beating heart.

No, be still my beating mind.

Heart, you go right ahead on.

The path to my heart is not clean. There are layers of protection. A pack of Dobermans sniff out any would be interloper seeking ingress. Thought, feeling, experience, or person. It's a process that's been working for centuries, and for *me*, in my seventy-plus years, to insure safety and survival. I've gotten better at relaxing the standards my fears set so long ago.

My heart now stands at the center of my being and my presence on the world. Not my mind. It could be the proximity of death, but I more readily leave the door to me open. The aortas to me. The expected flow to me from my life, or the foreign flow of another's.

These latter, transfusions to have me know the sameness of Self. This is all on my more centered days. Askew days, all bets are off. Askew days have me worrying about my physical heart and all its neighbors and how it's all going in the neighborhood. Like down on Liver Lane. Or focus on the just plain physical. Like shelter and income and food to eat in the 'hood.

It's interesting, and I hope healthy for me, in an overall way, to have my heart at the center of my wheelhouse now, and not my head. Good old reliable head. Maybe not so much. Especially as I'm beginning to forget my former addresses, the numbers on the houses (not the streets or cities yet, thank God), as well as why I walked into this room. It just seems like my *heart* is more reliable now, and the organ that plays best in the cathedral of my life. Being head/brain correct or "right" doesn't hold the promise it once did, for my ascendancy in the world.

I wonder how many of us have to get to 70 to recognize this wonderful truth and choice. Actually it looks like everything works pretty well till we're about six or seven, and apparently once again toward the end of the game. It's the 2nd and the 3rd quarter we have the most trouble with. Like worrying about using a preposition to end a sentence with.

If there was only one part of me I had to entrust my heart to, it would be to my child or my current me. "We" both trust and have trusted our feelings the most. Feelings, the beautiful, scary, sometimes unfathomable outpourings of the heart. *And* the most reliable gauge of the authentic. Honoring feelings has been the single best invitation I've given myself, to begin to lead an examined, awakening life. Discovering *my* emotional truths. Seeing that this is my main aorta connecting my physical self and universe with my formless and timeless Self.

Not unlike the keen smell and protective stance of the Doberman, I stand guard over and attend to this heart of mine, the once and future passenger/king, in the golden chariot of my life.

Beat on.

Earth Life/Scoreboard

In the game of life

We are both "Visitors"

and "Home."

Human.

And Being.

Earth Life/Scoreboard II

The game?

Peek-a-boo

I see you.

Hide and seek.

Now I see

Who I truly am

Now I don't

Now I do…

Vacation: New Mexico

Come thou

magic mountain

winds

and whisper me

away from

duty work

teach me

know my isness

not my business.

★   ★   ★

This poem appeared originally in University of Louisville's *Thinker*, vol.14 # 1, Winter 1989–90.

Aspen Arbor

Red River, New Mexico. With Angel Fire and Eagle's Nest, a triangle of mountain settlements just out from Taos. Our first place to vacation in the West. After years of going to Carolina in more than just our minds, North *and* South, we changed directions when Michelle, our daughter, graduated from Murray State in Western Kentucky, and moved to Colorado. This year, in the mid-80's, after visiting her, we went to Red River. I had traveled a lot to the West throughout my first career. My commitment to being with my family left me mostly views inside schools, auditoriums, theatres, gyms, civic centers and churches. In many ways, this was the first time I would stop, breathe, and be with the West. It was a simple and profound experience.

We lodged ourselves at a cabin in the still-no-traffic-lights heart of Red River. Motoring in, in a moon-roofed van, was a constant splash of Autumn's deciduous wardrobe and high desert flowerings.

Both Maleita and I are by now visual artists. Me, beginning at 52. She, at around birth. The light of the Taos sun and the stage it got to illuminate was a sea change in our visual experience.

"Ooohs" and "Looks" abounded, followed by, and eventually re-placed by, extended silences. It was the beginning of a dance that would lead us to move from our 50-year home and terrain in Kentucky, to the West, landing in Sedona, Arizona.

Here in New Mexico, we were just beginning a two-week stay. We spent most of our first day in Taos Square, in galleries, pretty consistently alternating between inspiration and despair. Mostly inspiration. I already knew and surrendered that I wasn't Sargent or Picasso. We started the evening drive back up to Red River on a two-laner, already informing us through signage that we would be sharing the road with wandering cows. We were not disappointed. Several four-leggeds shared some part of the trek with us, or rather, we with them. The pace was laid back, if not altogether laid *down*. It was not unwanted. The land and sky and softening sun were conjuring up a day's finale. We decided to pull over. And get out. It was a place of vast expanse. We stood. Silently. With the cows. Until Taos' answer to the Northern Lights played itself completely, spectacularly, out. We clapped. It just arose.

★   ★   ★

Without plans, we found ourselves naturally alternating nature days with citified days. Our earliest hike was up Mt. Wheeler. Not up, as in to-the-peak up, but up, as in the highest our bodies would put *up* with. We "used" every bit of daylight, all our rations (of food and energy), and most wonderfully, all of our senses. Surprisingly still-green, lush bowers. Stutter-staired stream dancing its way down its steep, random bed. Rocks of ages and beauties and sizes galore. A high-mountain clearing and lake, festooned with the finest fall flora that Gaia could give. Wonderland.

My body surrendered quickly and easily that night to deep sleep. The rest of me was not tired, and took me in dreams, up the very same path. A double feature.

★   ★   ★

Greenie Peak. By Jeep. Nothing in that combination sounded scary. The Jeep wranglers (that is to say Jeep renters) were laid back in the extreme about degree of difficulty, and even about where to begin. We presumed the Peak was the place to end. Our bodies (altitude and endurance challenged) were quite ready for some *automotive* climbing. *And* it had rained at this lower elevation.

We mounted the Jeep, to continue the wrangler metaphor (it

was actually a Renegade), and I re-familiarized myself with 5-speed, manual transmission voyaging. We took our best guess as to where to declare point A and head up. A road would have been caviar. Well, not to me. Maybe fresh salmon. A path would have been a Kobe steak. What we found and kept re-choosing as a route, was pretty much Spam.

We slogged through soft, rain-soaked passages within the trees, and were sure this would be our best view of the trip, while we waited for a tow out to home. As the incline steepened severely—a rock bed appeared. It was the only clearing going up. Calling it a bed is a big, big misnomer given the enormous size and angularity of each now-slippery rock. Boulder bed, maybe. We were so grateful to have squeezed and churned ourselves this far, though it looked like Jacob's ladder. The ascent to heaven. Would there be wrestling? Oh, yes. For footing and traction. For calm. For gears and agile clutching. For not flipping over backwards and tumbling back down. For not flipping out. In the end, I am convinced the angels that day were not there to wrestle us, but to see us safely to the top.

And what a top. A peak with no peak. More like an open meadow. White white with virgin snow and air. Flecked extravagantly and just impossibly with magentas and saffrons and lavenders and ceruleans. Who could believe these floral presences in such rare air? We stood ankle deep in the white, and let them be the villagers and dancers of this momentary, timeless home.

The ladder down and pathway home to the wrangler's corral was quiet, somehow easy and suffused with afterglow. Another wordless experience. Gift.

★   ★   ★

Nothing could have prepared us for the Santa Fe Opera. I knew it was outdoors, but not exactly how that might look or feel. I am not an operafile. I didn't know that *La Traviata* had no memorable melodies (at least to me), and that nothing actually happened in it except between acts. Well, there was a death on stage, but it progressed so slowly, it was hard to call it action. I love arias. I've heard many. Never lighted on a favorite female. Callas and Sutherland and Fleming would be in the running. Prefer male singers in this genre. Caruso was cool. I was impressed with and moved by Pavarotti. I *love* Bocelli. Arias. Pop songs. The phone book. I just connect with the way he connects with the music and lyric. Saw him once live with the San Diego Symphony. I didn't wash my ears for a week.

Here, though, in Santa Fe I couldn't have known that the most moving and heart-connecting experience would happen in the parking lot. We arrived super early to allow us time to just experience the venue, and maybe a sunset. The sunset dropped out of the program rather early, curtained by a grey and drizzly sky. We remained vanned as we knew our tickets weren't under roof. Others began arriving. The lot was starting to fill. The sprinkle was light and intermittent. The first time it hesitated, several vehicles began to empty their human cargo. Elegance would not be a superlative. The humans extracted more cargo. A van parked right in front of us. It joined the pattern. But not completely. This vehicle was equipped with a lift out its side, and presently, a frail white-haired man, wheel-chaired, was being mechanically lowered to the ground, attended by a younger, abler man. Next, the card table. We looked around. Several card tables, by several cars. Back to the two men. White linen. Crystal. Silver. Silverware. Tapered candles. The sky began to mist. The abler man brought out a bottle of wine and an umbrella. He served his seated partner and stood steady over him with his protection and care. His own setting went unused. We began to mist. A fine aria.

Operatic "tailgating." Who knew? With this one inveterate sports fan moved beyond words by the "action" before the curtain.

★   ★   ★

When our last day in the West dawned, our hearts were already heavy. I was surprised at how I avoided even picturing going home, to the East, to Kentucky. Not that I didn't love beautiful Kentucky and my lifetime of friends there. I was refreshed by our vacation. Re-created. I just didn't want to leave.

I laced up my shoes for a morning run. Maleita coffeed up for her walk. Our cabin seemed to be an epicenter radiating endless forest runs. Having no well worn, clear paths, everywhere seemed the road less taken.

I bounded out. Clear air. Soft ground. Ready legs. The evergreens and Aspens swiftly enfolded me. Let me do my dance between them, while they did the slow one with the turning earth. All of us doing our fast one with bright energy flashing inside us. Pumping along goes my frame. Canopied and safe. Zig when it opened. Zag through a slat. Over a log. Downhill a bit. Sunspots appearing. The Bright One woke up. Dappling my on-again, off-again path-of-the-day. No-tension ascension, clean burn on the level, body and spirit forgetfully one—a clearing. Small, but a clearing. I stop dead. I have entered a space, the home of a half dozen Aspens. Standing blindingly tall in a circle. And yet not. There is one empty spot in this symmetrically perfect circle with equidistant beings, all save for that one. Without hesitating, I step into the circle, at the space that invited me. The vacant place. It is impossible for me to describe in words the next few, or many (I don't know) minutes. As soon as I "clicked" in place, this vast peaceful awareness enveloped me, was me. Oneness. Communion. Suffusion of sure-hearted knowing no separation from anything that exists. I believe I stood for some time with *my* branches extended toward the arms of my Brothers and Sisters. I believe I gazed for some time up the cone, the golden ring of sun-spattering, wind-partnered, jitter-jogging leaves.

I don't remember leaving. I *do* remember a new feeling about my place in the family of things. I *do* remember getting to the cabin first. We had taken very different routes every day. As today. Maleita opened the door. She looked glowing. She opened her mouth, twice. She spoke slowly, "You'll never believe what just happened to me." Space. "There was this circle of trees…not really a complete circle…"

We ate breakfast and packed, mostly in silence. Much later, in the afternoon of the first day's drive East, somewhere in Texas, Maleita said, relative to nothing and to everything, "It feels like they're saving a place for us out here."

Four years later, we took it.

★　★　★

I'm in the tree

The tree is in me

I feel the life of life

in veins and limbs flowing free.

We reach out our arms

We welcome our friends

Each day the loving circle grows

the Dance has no end.

a verse in the song: "Plant me a Tree," by Joe Wise.[13]

★　★　★

"There is a synergy in the Aspen Grove. The trees are connected by a system of roots; each tree draws strength from the others. The grove is more than the sum of its individual parts—one plus one equals three or more."

The 7 Habits of Highly Effective People
by Stephen R. Covey[14]

Coming to Sedona

Landing in Flagstaff. Meeting with two Franciscans who invited me. Being driven down the 89a switchbacks. Becoming more and more aware of what was outside the station wagon. (It was the mid-60's). Being asked what the schedule would be for the retreat I was asked to facilitate. Stunned by the first full red rock vista. Forgetting to breathe. These are my memories of first placing my toe in the ocean of Sedona. And it was an ocean. Twice. Dry now. Enough, but not so much that it couldn't become a mini Grand Canyon you could *live* in. Which I was about to do for two weeks.

My answer to my hosts was, What little I have planned just changed. Most, no, *all* of the afternoons would be free so I could "get out in this." They smiled a Franciscan smile. I became aware Francis might well have called this place Brother Canyon, Sister Stream. The current locals called it Oak Creek Canyon. Nothing in me could name it.

My first afternoon took almost forever to arrive. I struck out with meager supplies and ample heart. There was no other building in sight. The ranch I was leaving nestled in the heart of an area now called Back O'Beyond. As we drove through Sedona coming in, I could recall seeing only a dozen or so buildings. The Village of Oak Creek, now a thriving community, did not exist. Wilderness, desert, and a kaleidoscope of Red Rocks stretched out before me. They became the entirety of my world for some unknown time.

Drawn by a formation of great height from the desert floor, I hiked to its base and began a climb. I was in my twenties, which

The Truth in Twenty ... and Then Some   189

helped both my daring and a few extreme purchases. Topside, I stood breathless. And breathless. For the first time in my life, my vision was not wide enough to receive what mother earth proffered. I sat. Choosing the vista with the most formations. I settled. Holding myself back from overwhelm. I breathed.

Everything that I could see rising up from the floor—red, shape, rock, shape, limestone, shape—stood in beauty and vastness and song. Altogether perfect conduits of their infinite, formless Source. I found myself equally delighted by its endless iterations, and silenced by its totality. It remains one of the strongest moments of physical awe I've known.

Just before my descent, in my last sweep of a relatively neighboring formation, I noticed an odd escarpment. I could almost believe I saw a building. Or part of one? People see mirages in the desert. This one looked like 2 or 3 miles away. Down I went and across the floor. My curiosity about my destination was interrupted many times, by my wonder and surprise, at all the varieties of flora at my feet and knee, on my chest and head, and even above. Bushes from my mountain, were trees.

An opening.

I stand at the base of a cliff, *and* a building. Both jutting out together to form a face. A spiral stone walkway leads up. I take it. I see no one. I round a curve. This is a chapel. Cut right into the rock. Simple. Majestic. I step in. The stone triangle rises far. A few more steps. I see the glass wall in front of me opening me and this edifice to the beauty of The Canyon.

I hear a sound

hidden speakers

It is *my voice*

I stand alone in this space

and hear songs from my first album

only three months old

No one even knew of it...

Yes

they did.

A moment.

★ ★ ★

I was invited back the following year by the Franciscans, before they moved away. Then Brother Canyon and Sister Stream began their invitations directly. Twenty years later.

Maleita's affair began in the mid-80's. With Sedona. It lasts even to this day. Sedona loves her too. She has been in countless publications with her prize-winning art, her unique and sought-after teaching skills, and her persistent generosity. As I write this on the eve of her sixteenth birthday in Sedona, she is pictured and featured in the weekly magazine *Kudos*, among those designing, decorating and painting cups to be sold as a benefit for Gardens for Humanity.

Maleita's humanity first encountered the garden of Sedona through a change in the default setting of our vacations. It had been the Carolinas and the ocean till Michelle, our daughter moved to Colorado. Now it is the West. In '86, after we explored New Mexico for a couple of years, Sedona returned to my consciousness, and I asked Maleita if she had a preference for a post-Michelle destination. No. Well, then, there's this sleepy little town in Arizona. "It's pretty spare."

"That's ok."

I brought her in the same way I had come, down from Flag, winding through Oak Creek (the) Canyon. "Oh my God's" found her lips, as soon as her soul received the first retinal transmissions of red rock formations, at Sedona's edge. My own 23-year absence left me just as helpless, and unable to pay any great attention to the pride of "discovery," or even the joy of sharing. There was just the electricity of her, Sedona's, presence. Her singular wedding of warmth and majesty, intimacy and vastness.

The town was larger. More populated. More commercialized. Predictably really. Yet with each return, we lamented a new traffic light. More stores. Everyone who's loved Sedona wants to be the last one in. But who would I leave out from the mix I would also come to know as Sedona: Larry? Sandy? Paul? Melissa? Charlie? Cathy?. . .

For now, we settle into our A-frame rental, and let our high stimulus settle into something approaching homeostasis. It is a pleasant procedure. After dinner, we find ourselves at the Chamber of Commerce, thumbing through stands of activity brochures and leaflets. I come across a medicine wheel offering. Then a second. We talk. We would both like to experience this. The third features guides trained by Sun Bear, of the Oglala Sioux. I had facilitated a retreat with him some years ago in Kansas. I liked his wedding of spirituality and earthiness. We call. We are on for tomorrow morning. We would meet our guide near a market at the "Y," Sedona's only major intersection.

Sleep came easy that night. Alertness and expectation rose with the sun. The market was easy to find. The guide wasn't. She was on time. In a vehicle, it turns out, with no markings. A surprising ribbon of ingress and egress had materialized at the market. Everybody is up early in Sedona. Eventually I find one person who is standing quietly and still. "Are you waiting for people to do a medicine wheel with?"

"Are you Joe and Maleita?"

"Yes."

"I am Jill. We can go."

We climb into a van as scruffy as Jill. She is slight, but wiry, and I suspect is surprisingly strong. She would be on a short list at central casting for "mountain woman."

"The brochure said up to ten people."

"You're it."

I am glad. I will feel freer. We begin our long ride up a short road. Schnebly Hill Road. Why it's called Schnebly everybody knows. It's Sedona's last (married) name. Why it's called a *road*, nobody has a clue. It is deeply rutted, hopelessly eroded, sprinkled generously with boulder-sized rocks and contains within the confines of *itself* many opportunities to misalign your vehicle. Many have returned from Schnebly, rejoicing they have incurred "only" minor damage.

Jill is skilled. I relax. A little. And begin to welcome new vistas as we rise up from the canyon floor.

"Where are you from?" I initiate.

"Tennessee,'" says Jill.

"We're from Kentucky." More ruts.

"What part of Tennessee?" I re-initiate.

"Nashville."

"That's our home away from home."

"How so?"

"I've recorded a lot of my music down there and have many friends. Some I call good and even best."

"My brother was a priest there."

"Was?"

"Yeah…he got married."

"How long ago was that?"

"Maybe 15 years or so."

"I only know one priest down there and *he* got married. Bucky Jackson was *his* name."

"He's my brother."

Maleita and I look at each other and she says just a beat ahead of me: "We sang his wedding."

"It's where I met John Pell," I say.

"I met him," she says, dodging a boulder.

John is a best. Together we've traveled and performed in several countries, produced almost two dozen albums, walked through Dachau, celebrated each other's children, helped each other through some mid-life crazies, been privy to shared hilarity and heartbreak, and all the nameless little moments that assume their true, endearing place in your life-picture with enough time. I would have known none of this, or him, without this woman's brother, and his decision to leave the priesthood and get married, inviting both John and I, along with Maleita, to provide the music for his brave heart's decision.

I am feeling even more relaxed about the Medicine Wheel and my level of participation. I was approaching it as a sacred ceremony and a space for personal revelation, release, and transformation. I feel at a crossroad.

I ask Jill why and how she came into this work, this ministry. She shares a brief but naked picture of her path to here. Some segments are not unlike the experience of the road she is navigating as she speaks. Maleita and I contribute our journeys to the growing pool of trust. Jill adds she has been praying to have participants who would take this with intent and purpose, with heart. I am that. I am ready.

The overlook she takes us to is broad and wide, yet somehow intimate. We walk out to the edge. Breathless. Stillness. The vistas here are *truly* magic. All the families of red rock formations are present here, all the strata, all the shades. They form a crimson corridor canyon falling away right down to Sedona, the people part of Sedona, and include an other-worldly series of giant saucer rocks, on the intervening floor. Cathedrals could only aspire.

Jill calls us to the assembly of three. We have brought water and hats. It is July. In addition she brings a small leather-covered book, a transparent bag of white feathers, a pouch of tobacco, and a packet of rolling papers.

We are to gather rocks from the nearby environs to use in the assemblage of the wheel. I like the "wheel" in "Medicine Wheel" because of its suggestion of movement, as well as its pointing to wholeness as a circle. I want to feel whole and I want to move. Not physically, I don't think. I am laying down a unique and thrilling career for the sake of my soul, and trust in its inner guidance, and now want to move out of the bardo, the in–betweenness, the unpluggedness that I feel with great discomfort. The career was so unique it had my name literally on the ticket, and the albums. And who am I, if I'm not that? How subtle its connection to my sense of wholeness, identity.

"There are many elements to the wheel," Jill says as she begins her priestly part. "The seven directions. North. South. East and West, Above, Below, Within." I resonate with the "within" as a direction, as a dimension and reality included so naturally with the world of the seen. "Placements and constructions," she continues, "meditations and speech, stories and parables, de-construction." We have entered the two-hour ceremony. Our pile of rocks are slowly placed in circle and spoke pattern. Pivotal, especially intersecting, stones are placed only after meditation on the parable that it will represent in the wheel. Whoever connects most to its content will place it. Strong connection is symbolized by placing a white feather underneath that stone. In the deconstruction, as we move our stones back to their more random places, we will leave the white feathers. Eventually, after we leave, the wind will lift them up and carry them heavenward. This is our confirmation that the Great Spirit has heard us and received our prayer.

The one parable I most fully remember was of Turtle. Among turtles. Traveling overland. Jill reads from the small leather book. They fell prey to many predators. One among them heard a call to transform. Radically. There would be many difficulties for him personally. He answers yes. Begins. Becoming a creature of great size and plumage—an elegant, powerful soaring bird. He now can see his tribe and their path more clearly. He can now see predators approaching and give warning. Indicate alternate paths and havens.

Jill closes the book and we sit with this story. I am overcome with this creature's great courage. To leave the familiar. To do it alone. To look like he was abandoning his family, his tribe, his kind. I begin to weep. And then to speak about where I am. What I am afraid of. What looks lost, including me. I place the rock. And a feather.

Jill declares a break and she goes under a scrub tree just outside the East gate of the circle. We find ours near the West gate. Ample shade. Long drinks. I glance over at Jill and am thrown into my childhood on my Granddaddy's farm, watching her/him pouring tobacco in the trough of paper formed by a left forefinger. Closing the pouch with a free hand and teeth. Licking the length of the paper and rolling it round just right, finishing with a twist. Maybe she *is* a mountain woman.

I am distracted by a movement out on the wheel. A fluttering white bird. Looks like a dove. A stranger in the land of the giant ravens. Slight and white. Settling. Looking. Reaching under my Turtle rock and pulling and pulling and pulling out… the feather. He flies away with it—out over the canyon—down toward Sedona. On and on till I see him no more. Maleita and I slowly look at each other. I am so far outside my experience catalogue. We walk over to Jill, and I find my voice, and ask in as quiet a one as I can find, "Does this happen frequently?" She replies in a low monotone, staring after the flight path of the now-vanished bird. "I have not seen it. I have not heard it told."

It seems we are all moving in a different dimension now. Slowed down even further. More stunningly alert. As Jill directs us in the final stages of the Wheel. One piece of which, is to consider which of the quadrants, contains the stories and strengths we would most like to draw on. We sit in silence there, in that quadrant, for an extended time. I am trying not to be distracted by the dove. Not to focus on his choosing *my* Turtle feather out of the almost two dozen Maleita and I have placed.

I let it go. I quiet myself, to allow the medicinal, healing, encouraging effects of the Wheel to enter me, course through me, embolden my blood, purify my vision, open my heart. It does.

Jill says—one more short break and we'll start the put-backs. We go to our trees and drink. The quiet remains. The sky fills. In *front* of me it fills, with flash and flutter and swoop. Here is a *flock*, a whole wide *flock* of doves, all coming to our space, our wheel, to us.

I watch as they land. I watch as they seek. As they find. As they pull out each and every feather. One for each. Just enough for everybody. Then lift, together. In formation together—going high, high, high over the canyon.

★   ★   ★

I know we returned the stones. I know we came down from Schnebly. Jill probably did a thoughtless, artful slalom. A brief, focused good bye. I remember no words. I remember no time. I remember it was days before we could speak of this. And years, even up to this one, it blesses us.

Sequel to Schnebley

It would be several years before we followed the doves and flew into Sedona. And many visits. Once, after a two-week stay, we arrived back in Kentucky, a 55-year home, only to turn around two days later and come back.

In a much less elaborate personal ritual, we climbed a mesa held sacred by anyone who's stood on it. Its current name is Airport Mesa. It's where things arrive from the aether. Or where we raise our consciousness, alertness, and openness to receive. And decide. Which is why we were there. It was still a place known and frequented by few. No asphalt turnout marked its location. This day we are able to spend close to an hour there alone. It *is* a neighbor to the mesa that is now Sedona's small craft airport.

We began in conversation. The big pluses and big minuses in moving ourselves here. When that had played out, we felt ourselves at the moment of truth. Separating from each other and finding our own corner of the mesa, we would each decide. I went to the side that opened out toward Bell Rock, that chapel, and the Village of Oak Creek—though I spent scant time with that view, choosing to lay down and face the sky. Maleita chose the vista of Sedona, herself. After the magic of the doves, we were keen to the possibility of a sign. None came. We came together, both of us confessing we held out for a plane with a "Y" or an "N" in its identifying number on the fuselage or wing. There were only two take-offs and a landing. None of them sported a "Y" or an "N." We laughed at our mutual bail-out plan to let something else decide for us. In the warmth of that laughter, and following smile, we found, acknowledged, our soul's decision. Long before, really. Every time we left here, as Maleita said, "my soul stayed there."

So we began letting the rest of ourselves catch up. Finding a place. A place to build. Finding *the* builder. Finding that the house across the street from our lot was lived in by the builder's secretary. She asked us if we would like her to put a letter we might write to the house, in the poured concrete by the bedroom. Is this Sedona? Are all Sedona people. . .? We had already written, and hidden in the rafters, a farewell letter to our 22-year-deep-in-the-woods-treehouse-kind-of-home in Kentucky. We had a ritual with the new owners, which included a removal of our name and "Welcome" ceramic from the front door, a handing over of the key, and a passing of a small ceremonial branch—and with it the care of the woods—from our hands to theirs.

Our new community in Sedona was apparently as attuned as we were to marking transitions. When we would visit during construction, the grounds and rooms were never home to discarded items. The very first time we pulled up and got out of our car, we could hear clearly and at elevated decibels the carpenter's boom box playing—Vivaldi. "The Four Seasons." Echoing through the timbers and frames and footings of our new place of creativity and refuge. Taken aback would have been a good phrase to capture my reaction. Then, walking forward to meet the men, I had up to that moment, held in stereotype.

These same men would show up for me in my first public appearance in Sedona. I had submitted a slide to the newly formed Northern Arizona Watercolor Society, hoping to be juried into their premier show at the Sedona Arts Center. My piece was accepted. At the time of the opening reception for the exhibit, we had been three-week residents of Sedona. Who would I ask to be there for and with me? Who did I *know*? Who *did* I know? I knew the painters and the carpenters and the stucco people and the builder and the secretary. They all came. Some in their work clothes, fresh from their labors. I felt great. I felt grate-full.

It was a couple of years from that night that I pulled out the program and saw who the juror was for this show. It was Dick Phillips. I had since taken a workshop with him. Maleita had since given me a semester with him in Phoenix. Later she too came on board. Semesters extended into years. He became my primary painting mentor, and eventually my good friend. This Saturday I will read my tribute to him at his memorial. He passed a few weeks ago. It's still fresh to me.

As I write this, my mind lights on that first of hundreds of paintings I shared with him. The one that got here before me, the one he juried in to that premier show. The one I am thinking of with this moment's consciousness and meaning. It is of a man, seated, with a large suitcase and an even larger straw hat by his side. His sunglasses are on his bare knee. I called it "Tahiti by Tonight." It could have been "Sedona by Today." His was a vacation. Mine a sea change. He was black. And young.

But he was me.

9-12-11

Dick's Eulogy

Once in a while, or even once in a lifetime, if you are lucky, someone "appears" in your life as an inspiration, guide, catalyst, way-shower, at a moment you are ready to step into a new you. Such a person for me was Dick Phillips. Painter. Teacher. Mentor. Friend. Early in our move to Sedona, I took a one-day workshop with Dick. I came home altered. I told Maleita I had met my "teacher." He lived and taught in Phoenix. Well over 100 miles away. On my birthday, she gave me a semester with him, in a class with 14 other painters. He said, "He won't drive down here every Monday." She said, "He would." I did. Maleita came, and worked on her sculpture pieces in a neighboring classroom. One day, when only 13 others showed, Dick invited her into his class. She, too, was smitten.

He almost danced when he painted. He trusted the flow. Never even hinted anyone should paint like him. Helped us examine all the elements of art and composition, color theory and design. Then dove into a demo with no seat belt.

His memorial was large, yet warm. A lot like Dick.

"Easel death." A phrase born during my semesters with Dick. On the Letterman show, it would be the number one reason why you're not putting your painting up at "crit"[15] this week. The most sought after words in this procedure were his "Nice piece. Sign it here." We re-named a classmate's cat too. The edges of her paintings always had

*The Truth in Twenty … and Then Some*203

a ragged look, thanks to her cat's love of Arches 140 lb. watercolor paper. We christened him "Deckle."

There were many new things for me in Dick's class. Mostly my voice. Finding it. My painting voice. It looked a lot like my life voice. The one I found more fully in my 40's. Painting is a dialogue. You and the piece. Adjusting. Working with accidents, the unwanted. Making much of it up as you go along. Like jazz, get the big design down, the chord structure, then take off. Paint your riffs. Endless value studies, and thumbnail sketches, often suck the life out of life.

Pay attention to the pattern of dark/light/dark/light. It is the rhythm of this planet. Of our lives. What we'll pay *most* attention to is the place of most contrast. In *this* celebration, it's death or passing, and the chance for each of us to re-decide what we'll do with our earth days.

I rejoice that Dick chose to paint, and teach. And have lunch. Including several that ran rampant with hilarity at the Honey Baked Ham place, and we got looks like "What's in *their* Happy Salad?"

I have known few men who so closely resembled their talk. It was his walk. One of generosity. In every category I can think of. Extra lucky me, I had a mentor who became a friend.

I heard a man once, with a near-death experience, who said he saw a wall that pictures from his life went up on. Nothing but *his* kind and good deeds appeared. From all ages in his life. If he couldn't think of one, the Beings who surrounded him would remember, and flash it up for him.

I will be on Dick's wall. Whenever it shines. Won't we all?

I expect him to be one of *my* greeters at The Gates. "Nice life, Joe. Sign it there." Nice life, Dick. You've already signed it here (in my heart). . . and here (in all us gathered).

Signage

I run a lot at Mingus High School track in Cottonwood. The teams are known as the Marauders. Their name is written, painted into lanes three and five of their state-of-the-art synthetic track, circling or ovalling a manmade playing field. The words are at the 50 yard line on both straight-a-ways. Mingus Marauders.

Now who wouldn't want a part of that? Every time I run over the words, I try to pick up a little more of the spirit of a Marauder. A taste for adventure. A ride on the high seas. Salt in my beard. Wood for a leg. Well, maybe it's not *all* rosy. But there *is* the element of at-homeness with mischief and risk, and mixing it up with the dark side. Or as Mark Twain said it:

"Now and then we had the hope

that if we lived and were good,

God would permit us to be pirates."

Last week a sign painter showed up to change the rallying cry, the slogan, the mantra for this year's Marauders. It goes in a big circle on the side of the grandstands. I see it clearly every time I come out of the scoreboard turn.

The painter began by painting out last year's offering: One Beat. Over my five miles he completes this year's: All In.

If you could say there are particles in the atom of Eckhart Tolle's teachings and reminders, then these are surely the heart of *The Power of Now* and *A New Earth*:

One Beat.

All In.

Coming and Going

Our first trip to Kentucky, after we had settled in Sedona, was colorful, especially at both ends. It was Spring, and Louisville offered up its bouquet to us: bounteous azaleas, poppies and tulips, daisies and daffodils, cherry blossoms living upstairs—all this couched in the lush and verdant greens Kentucky gave as bed.

It was the bouquet of our *friends* we traveled for. Family friends. Friend friends. We had taken care to see each and every one before we left. For us. For them. Many tears. Big laughs. Wistful smiles. Some surprised us. A cousin and his wife truly celebrating our adventure by owning an opportunity they had for a similar move, and let it pass. A few felt brave enough, safe enough, to tell us they were mad at us for leaving. I count this among the deepest of intimacies. Not-a-blue-ribbon-kind-of-feeling honesty.

I remember talking with a good friend of Thomas Merton's (the Seven-Story-Mountain monk from the Trappist Monastery in Kentucky) telling me the first thing she had to do when she heard he passed, was to forgive him for dying. Partly for the manner: stepping out of a shower onto a fan's electric wire in a country not known for appliance safety. But mostly to forgive him for leaving. This was about a month before I was on a panel with Elizabeth Kubler Ross. The combination gave me a key to emotionally clearing a death, a leaving-me in my mid-twenties by my then best friend. So young. Sled accident. Misread injury/wound. Lockjaw. I was, all of a sudden it felt, beyond my sadness, and angry at how young he was. At the sled. At the interns and the doctors. At the crazy disease that trumped a lifetime of vaccinations. At him, at last, for leaving me. The sadness came rushing back in to mix with the anger and the joys with him, and I felt as complete as I ever could (which is to say never fully) in my grief. I named my son after him.

Leaving by definition always has two sides. On this trip, I/we were the leavers. From my side in this equation, I had wanted to make clear to those who remained, continued in Kentucky, that my going to Sedona was not *at* them, but *for* me. And the sadness we melded in was the parting. No matter the future calls, letters and e-mails, we were parting. It was the joy of where we were going that made this even possible. As the traditional folk song, "Fare Thee Well," says: *It's not the leavin' that's grievin' me, but my true love who's bound to stay behind.* Our true friends who're bound to stay behind.

The one I saved for last, then and now, in this writing, was Eric. The friend I grew to feel most at *home* with. The friend I grew to feel the most home with. Through the vagaries of self-employment. Through the bravery of art, of showing up at the blank page, of raising children, of handing them over to people we don't know, who say they will love them. Through the rising and falling fortunes of a certain Kentucky university's basketball team. The blue one. Not the red one. When I left, I had a mutual friend help me show up at U.K.'s season opener by placing a life-size Fedex/Kinko's cardboard me, in my usual spot, at the end of their couch. In my Kentucky sweats. Seated position. I later received lots of snapshots of cardboard me in various scenarios around the house. Some, several, almost *all* relating to johns. He and Margie showed up for me when I was changing careers, and moving from solo concerts in auditoriums and theaters, to group readings in small, folding-chair poetry rooms. It is their house we are staying at now, making our forays out to see other friends, returning home at night. Unconditionally safe and loved. Some part of this move for me, subconscious for sure at the outset, was to see if there would be some people for me, *wherever* I went. It made the Wehder's house, home, a perfect base.

Back in Sedona, I already had a rapidly filling mid-sized box of letters from Eric. It, the box, has companions now. Our phone carriers are wealthy.

We say good-by again. I know the times I'll get to spend physically with him will be few, unpredictable, and precious. I hope he feels that in my hug.

★   ★   ★

The flight to Phoenix was divided, with less time and heart on the leaving *from* and more on the going *to*. Our space and people were waiting. Our van was too, in the long-term parking lot. Driving through the ninety miles of desert, with no billboards, vestibuled us. Ten miles out from our new home, a rainbow appeared in the sky. Many celebrate it as a promise of no more destruction. Another chance to build and grow. Some believe it points to wealth and precious things. We watched as one end of it took up residence, on our dash, inside our windshield. It moved *with* us. The other end stayed stationary right over our Village. Our end stayed with us, through all the turns, to the very last street, when the rainbow completely disappeared.

★   ★   ★

We sat a while in our driveway. There *would* be a wealth of things for us here. There *would* be some ones, *here* for me. All in color. Precious. New. Different shades. Same Light.

Capistranos and Sarahs

Of Geese and Men

It sounded like a truck

with a squeaky wheel

and it was only when it didn't

get closer or farther

that I thought to turn around

and

nothing

a quiet mini–mall parking lot

What else?

Then as much in distraction

as anything

I glanced up

into the clear

November sky

and there they were

scores and scores of them

Canada Geese

honking and swirling

flocking and reflocking

this was not an urban sight

I told myself.

Were they lost?

    Hey weren't we supposed

    to meet at Oxmoor?

    South is this way people!

    Says who?

    Says me!

And slowly the why of the circling

appeared on the northern horizon

wee pepper specks on the bleached

city skyline

a holy host of gamely geese

outstripped on the trek

by this brood overhead

came flailing and honking

their way to the pack

and as soon as they entered

the rosary of swirls

off they went in formation

a V,

the big wedge with the leader

at point and the rest draughting

nicely away to the South.

★　★　★

Miniature penguins

there were hundreds come in

from the sea that lay

right off this park

in southeastern Australia

a sight they were truly

and sound more than sight

here at dusk every day

a flotilla of fun

they emerge all at once

crystallizing their form

from the amorphous waves

waddling and faddling

dancing and babbling

reclustering beachside and

looking to sea

Boy it was a cold one

out there today, wasn't it?

Yeah, is Curly in yet?

Fooling with a starfish

last I knew.

Waiting they were

Joe Wise

for the last little guy

and as soon as he showed

they moved in a trice

bob-wobbling off to their

burrows, good night.

★   ★   ★

And who taught us

of leading and draughting

(are there Blue Angel genes?)

who schooled us in circling

and flocking, in headings

and courses, waiting

re-flocking, watching and waiting?

★   ★   ★

My kinfolks have circled

my grandfolks have circled

my friendfolks

my soberfolks

all of them circled

and waited

for me

all of a feather

for me

out of the blue

skies

for me

out of the briney

for me

circled surely and sweetly

for me.

I give thanks.

★   ★   ★

My reference here is to the biblical Sarah, and the use of her, and of Jacob, as paradigms for feminine and masculine spirituality. Joan Borysenko observes: " *'Climbing Jacob's Ladder' is based on the model of doing successive linear practices to accomplish communion with God. Bottom steps of the ladder may be moral precepts such as the Ten Commandments. Then come certain prayers or meditations meant to deliver you from one step of the ladder to the next. This is a beautiful model. It fits men and, since both male and female aspects exist in every person, at times women may find themselves climbing Jacob's ladder.*

But for the most part, women walk Sarah's circle. If climbing Jacob's ladder requires stepping linearly and doing work, Sarah's circle is relational and spontaneous. Everyone and everything co-exist in the circle, and God is at the center. Because of this circular relationship, you can't tell where one presence begins and another ends. You don't have to climb a ladder to get to God; all you need do is connect with the life that exists in the circle." In an interview with Carol O'Sullivan, at Gaiam Life (www.life.gaiam. com).[16] See also www.JoanBorysenko.com.

The wedding of the two spiritualities is celebrated by (no surprise) Pete Seeger, in his anthem/hymn, "Jacob's Ladder."

We are climbing Jacob's ladder

Brothers, sisters, all.

Every rung goes higher and higher

Brothers, sisters, all.

We are dancing Sarah's circle

Sisters, brothers, all

Every new one makes us stronger

Sisters, brothers, all.

A Bridge in Time

How terribly strange to be 70

Paul Simon released these words in song in his 30's, and mine. Seventy not only looked strange from where I was then, but actually *impossible*. I had trouble thinking of *anybody*, especially male, in my extended family that made it that far.

The song, entitled "Old Friends," came back near my 70th birthday in the form of a gift from my son, John, and a first release of the live recordings of a 1969 tour. Simon and Garfunkel. Old friends. Since 6th grade. With breakups and brief reunions, publicly and privately, even till the advent of 70 earth years.

I was in Nashville in '69 at Columbia Studios, recording an album called "Sweet Water." At the end of one long re-mix session, before we completely called it a day, or night, really, our engineer/ producer Mike Figlio, who had worked with "Paul and Artie," came into the engineer's room after a break, with a blank white-labeled 45. It helps to be near 70 to know what a 45 was. In the sound world, of course. Not the cowboy world. He said, "They just sent this to me." I guessed from Columbia's N.Y. studios. "Want to hear it with me?" Maleita and I were already huge fans, which only marginally describes the soul connections we felt toward these two. Yes, we would. He threw a few switches, to connect a turntable to the two mammoth and articulate Jensens, on either side of the listening console. We sat on a couch directly behind him. He said, "They think this will be the title track of their new album, due out in a month or so." The little vinyl disc filled everything in the room. Our hearts. Our souls. Our eyes. It was "Bridge Over Troubled Water."

The aftermath of silence felt completely natural. The nothingness felt complete.

Later, hours later, Maleita and I shared that our first *thinking* moments in the quiet were filled with: "What was *that*?" And further away from the quiet brought: "*Who* was that?" On piano, for instance, generating phrases that were so integral, it became impossible to think of the piece without these as essential markers in its DNA. It was Larry Knechtel, of course, among other things known for his L.A. session work, and eventual membership in Bread. For that moment of first hearing, he was a messenger who bridged soul to spirit.

And as fate, and gift, would have it, I was working with Fred Carter Jr., on *my* album. Their (Paul and Fred's) "The Boxer," included on the collection, had been released as a single months before. Fred plays the distinctive finger-picking style that is the heart of the track. He played his "baby Martin" on that cut—and on one of mine.

I met Fred in the parking lot at the studio. He was driving a pickup from his farm outside Nashville. He pulled two guitar cases out of the bed of the truck and started in. I said, "Can I help?" Meaning take one of those in his hand. He said, "Sure," and nodded toward the truck. I looked in the bed, and saw it would take several trips between us. I said, "How come you brought so many?" He said, "I don't know what you're singin' yet." I'm thinking, *Is he going to make up what he plays and how he plays it, on the spot?* Inconceivable. Not for Fred, a simple man, in the very best, enviable sense. All our takes were "ready" after the simplest of run-throughs.

Mike later told me Paul and Artie felt Fred's contribution to the Bridge album was so singular, that they gave him their eventual gold record for the album.

Meanwhile, I, too, had brought *my* guitars. All two of them. In the middle of the first run-through of the first song, I stretched my leg below my stool, feeling around, and quietly scooted my guitar cases under what I hoped was a dark space behind me.

Time it was and what a time it was, it was

A time of innocence, a time of confidences.

Forty years ago on that stool. Lots of innocence still. And a lot of confidence. The world of music and people to share it with was opening out before me. Most confide*nces* were still ahead. Life had not cracked me open that fully yet.

The friend who gave me my first listen to "Old Friends" was a relatively "new" friend, who felt like an old one. Tom. Strange how some people we meet feel so familiar and comfortable. Maybe we traveled together in another lifetime. Maybe. . .

Long ago, it must be, I have a photograph

Preserve your memories, they're all that's left you.

We had begun our photo albums. He even had a 16 mm. movie camera. The birth and early days of our children recently appeared in my mailbox on a DVD he had transferred the film to. When he played it, back then, he had put a simultaneous "soundtrack" to it, including the "name song" of our two firstborns. "Michelle," from the Beatles for mine. "Jennifer" (Juniper) from Donovan for his. I sang them both to myself as I watched this time. We both knew in the christening, as with a ship, they would sail their own seas. But that was far, far away from this moment. They have both christened their own baby ships.

Old friends, sat on their park bench like bookends

I don't recall us sitting on many benches in the park. I have no digital prints from those days. Digital was only a hand description. Some hard copy. But mostly heart copy. Many of this last, of us, with long sticks, taking turns, hitting a tiny white sphere, in converted pastures, and unconverted woods. Gratefully there is no soundtrack to some of these adventures. ("There Must Be Fifty Ways to Leave Your Driver").

I do recall us sitting on a bench by the river, having gone, it felt, as far downstream as this mighty Ohio—sharing our shock and grief over death's untimely reach into our pool of close companions. One we both knew, and one just mine. There was a lot of silence. We were nowhere near 70.

I have migrated to the other side of the country now. We both have migrated toward 70. I, in fact, have gone beyond "toward." Most days, as I write, run, and paint, 70 feels like most other years. Sometimes 70 feels like the new 90. Maleita and I also have signed a pact not to worry just because we walk into a room and say, "What am I doing here?" It *could* be a mature exploration of the philosophy of life. We remain grateful we have not yet put cornflakes in the coffeemaker.

Meanwhile, the park bench I sometimes share with my old friend is now a virtual one, in front of our screens and keyboards, 1,800 miles or so apart. This particular sharing I'm going to put in an envelope and mail to him. In all the unknowns of the home stretch, hard copy seems just right.

Spiritual Growth

Spiritual growth is a surprising oxymoron. We're always already fully "grown" spiritually. We just have to stop cultivating (mostly by noticing) the egoic chaff, and our wheatness "appears." It's the ongoing incremental appearings or awarenesses that make it seem like growth, rather than revelation, or pulling back more veil.

What You Want

It was naked, what she asked.
As naked as the baby, three months ago.
As naked as our admiration for the couple two tables ago.
As naked as the flowers I had entered in the show.

We were just coming from sitting the art exhibition down the road at Tlaquepaque. Mounted by the Sedona Visual Artists' Coalition. Of which we are members. *Free for All* is this year's theme and title. Sitting means basically hosting, and either opening or closing the gallery, depending on your shift. It is an invitation to mix and interact, tendered to each artist in turn, as we "sit," after whatever solitudes were ours in our creative run up to the opening. Sedona is an international mecca, and Tlaquepaque is a featured art and gift center. Maleita and I had met and shared with people from across the U.S. all afternoon, as well as had "surprise" visits from three souls we hold dear, in our our own zipcode and heartcode.

My piece in the show was of two wildflowers. Larger than life. Done in watercolor. All of it pretty much with single strokes of a big brush. Inviting myself to a "free for all" kind of painting. Trusting the process. I then made three or four different short-jar mixtures of acrylic colors and matte medium, picked up a fat balsa wood stick, and began to dip and throw, dip and drag, dip and blob, dip and smear the thick color soups all over the place.

It was different for me. My resident critics (you know, the committee in your head) weren't too excited. My wife, Maleita, was. I stayed open, leaving the piece in plain sight for days. What I was wrestling with became clear. This was the least thought and struggle and time I had ever placed in a painting. The one I felt least responsible for. The one, at last, for which I felt the least *control*. It was "given" to me. It was free. It felt from "All" and for "All."

I titled it "The Best Things in Life Are. . ." This is the statement I wrote, to be hung by the piece:

The moon

the mountains

the cliffs

the sea

the sun

and the clouds

the grasses

the trees

the field

and THOSE

WILD FLOWERS

The best things in life

are free.

For all.

Joe Wise

I wanted no clothing for this piece. No glass or reflective glare. Yet it *was* a watercolor painting, at base, and needed protection. Together with my framer, Trevor, I came up with hot-pressing my 140 lb. Arches cold-press watercolor paper on a board, with a frame (and wire) *all on the back*. With only clear, sprayed acrylic coats for protection, this "newborn" hangs, with no visible means of support, no visual border, and no intervening glass. Naked as the day it was born. A satisfying presentation.

A satisfying presentation is what we were looking for and expecting, as we approached our long-time-favorite eatery. No disappointment here, with a perennially popular hot turkey pastrami sandwich and a seasonal white cheddar and poblano soup. "Our" booth is warm. We are catching Sedona's last light. Our soup is little-Goldilocks' "just right."

The couple at the next table, senior even to us in our seventies, it appeared, were exchanging in high but thoughtful decibels. "*The King of Queens*," she says, looking up from her newspaper. "Now what *is* that? Was it a *play* on Broadway?"

"No," he answers, "I don't think so."

We both have another bite and begin to wrestle with whether to throw our voice and the answer across the small divide. We agree, it is *their* quandary. We talk about our favorites in the show. Who surprised us with their entries. How deftly everything was hung and displayed.

"Maybe it was a *novel*," she says.

"I don't recall a book like that," he comes back.

We both stop chewing, but we have too much in our mouths to say anything to anybody. Presently, we quietly observe once more this is *their* experience, and not ours. Our ideas for next year's show, and possible themes, rise up as accompaniment to the last parts of our meal, on a satisfying autumn evening.

"Was it that *movie*, with Basil Rathbone?"

That does it. It has now become an act of mercy. For all of us. And would absolutely save them from a fitful night of sleep. Up we jump to deliver, as graciously as we can, the antidote.

"It's a TV sitcom."

"Oooh," they both say. And *now, they* look familiar. We ask them where we might know them from.

"Perhaps you ate at *our* restaurant," she says, "when we were open, and you could taste the love in *all* our food." He tells us they were "Fournos."

We remember. It was our anniversary both times we went there, so I would have tasted the love in a frankfurter, but they and their food *were* singularly memorable. And they *were* the restaurant. He, the chef. She, everything else. They were the King and Queen of the outside-your-home dining experience. They say this is their second and "final" retirement. We thank them warmly for their gifts to us and Sedona.

We then begin to make our way to the exit, only to be "blocked" slightly by a baby carriage at the next table. We pause. This newborn is half asleep, half awake, perched, docked really, atop the carriage in a comfy baby seat at table height. I ask how old he is.

"Three months," the youngsome couple says together. I gaze at him. We lock eyes, as only, it seems, we of extreme age can. He, in his fresh knowingness. Me, in my growing, returning knowingness. Maleita concludes *her* connection with an out loud, "Precious." We nod to the parents, and turn to go, and the lady, alone at the next table, stops us with a gesture and fixes us with a strong, intentioned look.

"Would you call *me* precious too?"

Maleita, without hesitation, says, "You *are* precious."

There is a pause, while we both look at her with the same quiet as we did the last soul we saw. My eyes become full.

I break the silence with, "I admire you coming out and eating alone." She looks to be 40ish. In truth, I more admired her courage in doing what she had just done, than anything. I know, as I write this, I will call back this woman and this moment, any remaining time in my life I might dare myself to ask, for what I *really* want.

"It's not what I want," she says, "not the *way* I want it." She blinks twice. "But it *is* what is."

I say, "Amen." We nod. Me, with hands held flat together, palm to palm by my face, in honor and recognition. She nods.

The next steps we take put us at the door, and out into the clear, clean high desert air. I breathe deep. I feel full, brimming, gifted. I take Maleita's hand. Like my painting, I feel and know and place my trust in the Hidden Support. The part I see and the part I don't see. The same Hidden Support of aging Kings and Queens, of Fresh Infants and Lonely Hearts, of these recently blessed Artists and Sitters.

I look back once more through the large window into the bright, animated, close-tabled room, centered by an exuberant, way-larger-than-life, walloping spray and splash of great glass flowers, rising high above its diners. In perpetual bloom. A signature piece for its home, this restaurant, named—"The Wildflower."

Dharma Defrag

The complexity

    of my computations

keeps me

    from the simplicity

    of sitting.

Alicia, Landing

Immersion. That's what it is. We are in the Alicia immersion. Maleita and I. Part whirlwind. Part calm eye in the center. Everything in between. Big change. Big drain on senior bodies. Big rewards. Big love. Not so little Alicia. Eight, but certainly not little in any category. Four feet eight and one half inches tall. Five foot eleven wingspan. Uses every bit of it to soar through her life. Alighting for bed at 8:30. We at 8:31. *Her* process in retiring filled with trickery (spelled d-e-l-a-y) that a seasoned grifter would admire. *Ours* filled with simple collapse.

The other day, arriving at our old (her new) home after school, she put down her book bag and "soared" with arms extended, all around our main living space and canted: "I am a shooting star that's been landing in some bad places—now I am landing in peace." She came to complete rest in the silence. She is truly a grand, expansive child. Her stellar parents are re-focusing careers and location. We are the beneficiaries, also known as Gran and Papa, of her presence in this grand betweenness.

Yesterday her teacher at the down-the-roadway Waldorf School named Desert Star (what else?), confirmed what we've been seeing these weeks just passed. Entering at halfway in the school year, she is flourishing. As I left for my run this morning she was designing clothing. She has, in this brief sojourn, written an essay on creative imagination, begun an acrylic-on-paper equestrienne piece, composed a song for taking out the big garbage can weekly: "O Garbage Night" (think "O Holy Night" for seminal inspiration), learned to cartwheel, added two verses to a song I wrote in the 70's, read out loud with emotional accuracy and nuanced interpretation book one of the Lemony Snicket series, and conducted a druid-like peace ceremony at a local pond and park.

It was so soul satisfying to see how much her teacher, Sarah (Ms. Van Dam), "got" her. She shares from her child studies and her own examined life how the ninth year is about establishing yourself for the first time in and on the world. By definition, a time of great bravery and vulnerability. Releasing the comforts and presumed guarantees of "happily ever after" both in and around ourselves. Embracing the grit and the glories of this world *as it is*. Flaming forth a new, maturing, one-of-a-kind star.

The three of us, sitting in conference about her, feel honored and blessed and challenged. To foster her. To hold space for her. To *be* with her.

She *is* becoming less and less devastated when she ends up with the Old Maid, delights in beating me in our periodic morning dressing races (even as I remind her of the questionable glory of trouncing a 72 year old), and in random flashes almost daily grabs one of us, goes still, then rocks us gently with "I love yous."

Any or all pieces of this could be different. I am finding new levels and depths of gratitude within me. Or maybe it's me, it's we, who are in the Gratitude. Immersion. The fullest of Baptisms. We are watching her baptize herself into the world.

I Don't Do It

I don't do awakening

Awakening does me.

My part,

my pilgrimage

is to get closer

and closer

to my birthday suit,

make my way

to the shore,

stand expectantly

at the edge,

and wait

for High Tide.

And not be too

surprised

if this too

doesn't work.

Joe Wise

Tom, My Brother

I talked to my brother today. About cancer. About forgiveness. About moving on. The cancer is his wife's. The forgiveness was his. Moving on was all of us.

Less than a month ago, they had visited us for a week. 1,800 miles from their home, zero miles from mine, in Arizona. It was our first face-to-face visit in many years. Families and budgets and sheer distance played the tune we all danced to.

The diagnosis came a few days ago. Along with an email that said, "Wait for me to talk." He did, as I do, the inner quiet thing first. For me, it's finding if I can deal with this, even if I have no one—and there'll be a part of me who has just me.

The outlook, after more tests, grew a little less grim. Biopsies will follow and then a more targeted, specific protocol. We remembered when the word cancer, was worse than most curse words in our childhood and teens. It was not spoken. It was relentlessly synonymous with death. Now, happily, besides being able to voice whatever we need to, we find that therapies for cancer are growing, along with the ongoing discernment of varieties of cells. Many hopeful steps from the traditionally johnny-one-note song.

He had just begun the trip-of-a-lifetime, to honor and celebrate his love of restoring cars, taking one of his beauties on a multi-city tour. This, with his two sons and our other brother, who we call "other brother," thanks to our geographically separated, yet simultaneous experiences, of Bob Newhart's TV B and B.

Linda had had some health challenges recently, but this was a shot from nowhere, and, once announced, from everywhere. Tom turned before arriving at city number one. Together, they have begun the path of great unknowns and personalizing her care. As I told him how lucky she was to have him, he said, "I'm the lucky one. Both ways." He knew *I* got this. I live in the same blessed place with Maleita.

He thanked me for my card, when he got back to Nashville. We had had a conversation standing in a swimming pool, chest deep in cool water in torrid Arizona. It was about our childhood. I was the older brother then. Now, I'm "another brother," and, I hope, something beyond the "limits" of family, as he is to me. Back then it fell to me, and I chose to take care of him, champion him whenever I could. We were both (my assessment) greatly distracted and lost, though we couldn't name it then, in the dynamics of our parents' relationship. I began to tell him of my regrets for not being everything he needed or wanted back then. We were interrupted and the moment was "gone." I was finishing my part in the card by asking his forgiveness. In this call he tells me, "Already done. You can put this one away."

This, after a years-ago gift, following a round of golf together, with me on the freshman side of sobriety. Just off the 18th green, he put his clubs down and said, "I have something I need to say." I put mine down. He squared with me physically before he said, "I hated you for going to the seminary and leaving me as Dad's target." Our father was in the World War II generation, *in* World War II, and came home to the silent war inside himself. Triggered by his service, his experiences, his upbringing, eventual unsatisfying work, and the unmanly thing it would be to speak of any of it. The result was a man of great fidelity and sensitivity *and* eruptions. The last at small things. Usually things done by *me*. Then Tom. All exacerbated by his relatively unsuccessful and totally understandable dance with alcohol—a legal, manly peace.

I had left at age 12 for residential seminary training for the Roman Catholic priesthood. Tom left as soon as he could for the Air Force. The gift after the golf game was his honesty, his risk, his trust. He was the older brother that day. Part of the "no-talk" dynamic we were raised in made this the first day we spoke of these things. It felt extremely "disloyal" to me, yet deeply "right," and surprisingly peaceful in its aftermath. Mostly this day, though, I felt so sorry that this had never even *occurred* to me, the target thing. That I had, in essence, abandoned him. I cried. He cried. We fell into each others' arms. It was the most intimate moment I could remember in my family experience. The anger. The truth. The open-ended courage. The tears. By then, the group following us on the course, was coming off the 18th green heading to the clubhouse, and one of them said, "Was it that bad?" We both laughed into the tears and said in sync, "It was pretty bad."

Linda's diagnosis feels pretty bad. She and Tom have given generously, even into retirement, of their time and treasure and space to family. Their trip out here I saw as the beginning of a new chapter for them. A chapter where it was *their* time. I want so badly for modern medicine to have its way with these tumors, for the road to keep opening out for their delights in travel and custom cars, for the Source, the Healer of *all* Life to call her up and say: "Already done. You can put this one away."

★   ★   ★

Some months later Linda passed.

All in Calm

All in calm I sat

upon the bench seat on

my back deck feeling

quite at one with all the colors

and the trees my head

was in the sunlight

my knees within the shade

and only autumn's clime

could make me feel that line

cut sharp across my body

when all at once it happened

once it happened

once it happened

clang chime ring gust

cling clang and

dance in sudden

wind the mobile chimes

the clinging clanging

chimes while in the valley twixt the hills

the rain of leaves began

the clang, the yellow,

cling, maple, red, clang

chim, oak, chime, burnt sienna

clang chime spinning, ash whirling, red cling

brown, around chime, clang

yellow tumbling, red, gusting clang

gallery of souls,

going gaily off

to village green

called by church bells

to the place of unity

the holy humus

Joe Wise

plunging to their death

and life beyond

★　★　★

Originally appearing in *Chameleon*, vol.1 # 1, August, 1989

Right on Time

As I write this, Maleita is fashioning a bouquet of her tea roses. Marc Cohn's weathered delivery of "Right on Time" is still ringing in my ears and soul. It's from a gift CD by Jerry Douglas. From Cathy and Paul, two days ago. I played the cut for Maleita on the way home from the track this morning.

We ran late. Late is measured by when we arrive at Mingus High School's Bright Field, relative to the time the students arrive. When *they* do, *we* have to go. We were in the closer-than-ever waning moments of that window when I began my cooldown. This pre-stretch part is walking backwards, to balance and strengthen the front leg muscles and keep Mr. Shin Splints away. The studentless buses are coming from the main school building back to the parking area. Their path runs right beside the track for the width of an end zone and a half of a straightaway. It is unpaved. Dust abounds. I decide to, for the first time, do my extended reverse-walk in the other direction, away from the dust.

It puts me on a path of seeing a straggling student just outside the chain link fence. For about fifty yards we are "face to face." He is scrawny, short, slight of build, ipodless, looks like a freshman. It is Fall. He shuffles his feet along, looks down, and is talking to himself. Most kids are already in. He brings his eyes up quickly and hunches a little if he hears other students. I wave. I am not in his universe.

I have many angels. Some are presences I've known here, when they had human DNA. I ask one of them to attend to this boy today. To look after him in all his interactions. I could even release my oldest and dearest—who I call Johnny—for a day, if he was the best suited for this. My commission felt complete by the time the young boy disappeared through the school door.

Meanwhile on the same path, a groundskeeper, had rolled up beside me in a utility cart. I didn't know him. I know most all of them—from my years at the track here. He had stopped to unlock a gate he wanted through. "Hi," I say. He says, "Every time I've looked at you, I think you are my brother-in-law."

"Is he from here?"

"No. California." And as he pulls away, "He's a retired Blue Angel."

I feel confirmed.

In our own vehicle, I tell Maleita of my after-run events. She receives them, pauses, and says, "Reminds me. Let's stop by and see Kim. See how she's doing." Kim is the front-desk manager at the local Best Western. She was an angel for us one night last winter as we were seeking to prevent a homeless night for friends in another city. The last time we had dropped by the desk her friend Brian told us she had a life-threatening illness and was at the hospital. We visited. She cried. Even with complications from MRSA, she survived and returned to work. Today Brian again is on duty and tells us Kim received a call yesterday telling her that her father died. He paused and said: "How do you all know when to show up?"

We are wise enough to know this angelic network is not ours. Yet we *are* blessed players *all*, are we not? Messengers. Hearts. And hands.

Maleita is finishing the bouquet for Kim. Marc Cohn is still singing in me. Via Jerry Douglas. From Cathy and Paul. Right on time.

Running late. Right on time.

Buses in the dust. Right on time.

Backwards on the track,
   solitary boy,
   man who thought he knew me. Right on time.

The Rose Angel is ready to deliver.

This is *Blue* Angel, signing off for now.

Right on time. And still not retired.

★   ★   ★

Maleita reminds me as I read this to her that our *gifts* were running late. The ones from us to Cathy and Paul, and they to us—at a breakfast for birthdays and anniversaries, all gone past, "missed," this year. The *gifts*, of course, right on time.

I See You

She was naked. Lying on the floor. He was sculpting her. He wasn't surprised. He had told me to come to the studio. *I* was surprised. I didn't expect to see anybody but him. I felt awkward, invasive, even embarrassed. *I* had drawn and painted from live models before. This felt different. Like an intruder.

He quickly said, "Hi," and continued his work. Then she said, "Hi." I looked at her again and said, "Hello." I wanted to add: I didn't know *you* would be here. I was there to pick up a print I had offered for sale at a benefit. *Wait a minute. I know this girl, young woman.* The print hadn't sold, but several of my smaller works did. *Yes. Somewhere in the last couple of years I met her.* It was good of my fellow artist to pick this up for me. I couldn't be there for the event. *I know her from* Desert Canyon. *She was a client at the addiction center that employed me. I remember her now. I worked with her in group and watched her bravely own herself. All of herself. Deep and hard work.*

"It's over behind the saw horse, on the bench," he said.

"Thanks. Got it. I'll catch you later." I stride briskly for the door. I catch her eye one last time. "Good-bye," she says. With a subtle smile. I choose to believe it says, "We both know you've seen me way more naked. Thank you."

"Bye," I answer. Click the door softly shut. And say in a voice only I can hear, "Brave one."

In the End

In the end,

and the middle,

and the beginning,

there is never,

to give or receive,

a better

greater present

than Presence.

You.

Me.

All the way

There.

Here.

Out You Go

A writing experience from journal group. You see yourself as a soul, with 90 years' experience on this planet. Your passing over was rather recent. You are called on to briefly mentor a soul, who is about to be launched on a maiden journey to Earth.

Hello—Hello—How alike we look—It is good to see you and be here with you. Boy, have you got a trip ahead of you. It is so powerful and engaging you will forget who you are—often. For most, more often than not. But the good news is you will never cease—yes that too, now that I think of it—but you will never cease *being you*, even when you forget. It'll be like getting lost, but you'll always be found—even during the time you're lost. Time. Well. This is a biggie. This adventure wouldn't hang together without it. You will go through periods (two kinds if you're gonna be a girl), periods where time will take forever, and others where you just can't get enough time. The times that you forget time (that is one thing coming after or before another), you will be closest to remembering who you are.

Now *this* part is way cool. There will be others doing the same thing you are. It bumps up the randomness of your experiences. Adds some juice to the whole trip. If you're patient enough, you won't be able to tell what's good news and what's bad news.

Other way cool things are feelings—inside and out. You will touch things and you'll swear they are separate from you—this is usually one of the last myths to break. On the inside. Sometimes traveling to the *outside* will be all kinds of feelings. They will be the barometer for your level of engagement. They're also capable of great, even extreme range. They are definitely the cayenne of the chile. Chile. I won't even go into that. A later surprise—after pabulum. Basically they go all the way from fun to scary, and are a *big* difference in the way we are, when we take on a body.

Dying—huge experience—mostly before you get to it. Basically it's getting back to here. It is the opposite of birth, not the opposite of life—but because you forget so much—it's a crap shoot, unnh, a surprise. Since it's the last thing on the time line and you don't know when it's coming (unless you decide to purposely crash your car—er, your body)—since it's the last, it plays a part over and over in what you choose to do. Most of us have gotten *way* along the time line before we recognize and accept that we're only going to get *some* of the all. The only thing we all get all of, is our true Self and Elvis. Things that live on both planes.

I see you've chosen your parents already. They too will be *some* of the all. Don't expect too much of them. And be open to them being unwilling teachers. Don't underestimate their worth, however dark or light their teaching is. Much growth on this plane is through adversity, perceived differences, and pain (another component of the feeling grid I mentioned).

One other biggie that comes to mind: it's gonna feel like you are two selves, not one—at some point. This throws almost everybody. Into light or chaos. Or both. Most of the time they won't recognize each other, and the one you need only to drive your car, er your body, around will get off at the Death, or the Dying Terminal. Like everything else it's helpful to move out of adversarial relationship with the car self, the personality self—as soon and as often as possible.

Oooh—there's sex, not just like one of two kinds of bodies, but the two getting together—beyond cayenne, and there's singing and dancing, and silence, like now, only with stars. Oh, and there are peaches and cherries and mozzarella—well, I don't want to spoil the show—I leave it to you to be surprised like the rest of us when all these things appear on our path. Well, so long then. And look me up. I'm dying to hear what you learned. Actually, *I've* died so *you* could hear what *I* learned *this* time, on *this* planet. Back and forth we go, huh? Uh-oh. That was a contraction. Here you go now. Bon voyage. . . *Namaste*. . . so long. . .

The Innocence

In our "stories," our lives, our human experiences, we can never go back to "the Innocence."

In our being, we have never left.

Article in *Sports Illustrated*

A perfect combo for me. Sports and writing. In a magazine with high standards for "both." I had just decided to let go of lyric writing—as in songs—and taken up writing with no music—prose, poetry, monologues, short plays or scenes. I was really successful in the music career, but it felt "over" to my soul. I was feeling the fulfillment of writing in a new way, *and* missing a ready-made audience. A tough limbo at 50.

The piece came right out of my life. I was finding, and still do, my most natural ingredients and inspirations come right from my own life experiences. I have not as yet attempted, or felt moved to attempt, fiction writing.

It was my Sunday morning Church—once the league opened—a men's 45-and-over basketball league—at a local community center.

I went mostly out of curiosity. In 1989 I hadn't personally seen anybody over 35 playing basketball. I had been shooting on my own almost all my 50 years. Mixed in with intramurals and pick up games through college and grad school.[17] This particular gathering was a motley crew. Every build, every weight category, every caliber of excellence and ineptitude were fully represented. I was disappointed at first. I grew to love the experience. The prime rule was accommodation. Wait. Make allowances. Patience. Not unlike a great model for how to insert ourselves into the game of life.

★   ★   ★

Was it poetic justice/synchronicity where I found out? I picked up the mail from our rural mailbox on the way to the Center, and the gym. Threw it on the seat next to me till I pulled in the parking lot. Sorting through. Return address: *Sports Illustrated*. No big clue. I get periodic mailings and ads from them. I fingered it open. Two really short paragraphs. "We hope you haven't placed your writing on 45-and-over basketball with any other publisher." We want it. We want to pay you this (wow) amount.

The many poems and pieces I'd written, I had been submitting periodically for years to various places and journals. I had had only a couple of pieces accepted. Both poems. This was an extended prose piece.

I felt so validated, enrolled, blessed, received into the circle of professional writers. Affirmed to the max. Especially about my choice of material or subject. My own life.

I remember running in to the Center to the lobby phone and calling Maleita. Asked her to sit down. It was *that big* a deal to me. We both went nuts over the phone. She in the privacy of her own kitchen. Me in the publicness of the crowded lobby. One guy came up to me after I hung up and said, "Was it a boy or a girl?"

O boy, was it a baby of mine. Long after mine were grown. A new family. Born and blessed. Lucky lifetime.

Go, pen, go.

Aching for Basketball

Hoops for the 45-and-over set isn't the game you know

I had never heard of basketball for men 45-and-over. It sounded like a contradiction in terms, like "jumbo shrimp" or "military intelligence." I thought, What in the world would men over 45 do with a basketball once they got it?

I had seen men that old deal with the game only once, several years ago at an old-timers' game held the day before the NBA All-Star Game in Indianapolis. It was gross. All my retired heroes were on the court at once, panting and sweating, grunting and dragging their Buddha bellies (a fan's designation, to be sure) up and down the court until the merciful timekeeper buzzed them off the floor. They looked like *Wild Kingdom* answering the question "Where do the hippos go in the winter?" Thinking back on it now, I believe the median age on the floor was actually much younger than 45.

So what would mere mortals—amateur basketball junkies existing between their late 40's and Forest Lawn—do with the game if allowed to play? The question was important to me because I am a 50-year-old hoops junkie. It was prompted by an announcement that I read last year in the local community center's newspaper about a "Men's *Open* Basketball League." Three hefty columns gave all the pertinent information. There would be a $35 fee for the season. Right underneath that article, in three scrimpy lines, was a notice for 45-AND-OVER BASKETBALL, SUNDAYS 9 TO 11, NO FEE.

No fee. No money. No shirts. No referees. No timekeepers. No scorekeepers. No teams. None of the things the Men's *Open* League had. Yeah, and no *league*—just "basketball," on Sunday mornings. Making a commitment to play was not easy for a man who eats precisely one half a banana, one cup of skim milk and three fourths of a cup of oatmeal for breakfast every day, just to avoid the chaos of morning decisions. But I was prepared to adjust. I needed to play bad.

Although I had played mostly intramurals in my youth, I missed the roar of the crowd, the jostle of bodies, the contact, the sweat, the bite-squeak of gym shoes on hard lacquered floors, the picks and the rolls, the competitive edge—yes, the thrill of the game. Why I thought I would find this with men pushing 50, I don't know, but that should have been my first clue that I belonged with this group. My judgment was slipping.

These guys are not engaged in competitive activity. We guys are not engaged in competitive activity. What we are engaged in is hard to tell. But we talk about it every Sunday in the locker room. We come in to change and get started while the Men's Open League is coming off the court. We hear their bantering, "Nice shooting, Carl" and "Where the hell was our defense?" and "Boy, did you see Keith with that dunk at the half? He was airborne from outside of the foul line."

When we come in after our session, we talk about our prostates and hair restorers. I'm not sure whether this is due to short-term memory loss or because nothing really did transpire while we were out on the court. We come in and take off our jocks and wonder what we were protecting. In our group, which on a given Sunday can range from six to 10, everybody leaves on his warmup suit until we come back to the showers. We need that warmth to ensure circulation—all the way to the end. I was going to say until the fourth quarter, but I remembered we play until we have to give up the court—the games are seamless.

We use the same terms as the young men, but the words don't have the same meaning. For us, a fast break is an injury in the first

Joe Wise

two minutes. Our transition game is our walk from the locker room to the court. While circulation is one reason we leave on our warmup suits, another reason arose on our first Sunday. We decided that we would play shirts and skins as we had done as kids, so that we would know who was on which team. The skin team took off its shirts. The sight resembled a host of sagging Jell-O-like mountain ranges. Guys who didn't seem to have a bent toward aesthetics discovered that they did after all. That ended shirts and skins. Instead, we decided to tax our memories for team recognition.

We are a scruffy lot and like snowflakes—with the accent on snow—no two of us are alike. I think of Dan, for instance, as our leader, the focal point of what little cohesion we have. Dan is what's known as a gym rat. Dan is always at the gym. And he always wears the same clothes. They appear to have been made in the 1930s. Dan is in his 50's. His one nod to modernity is a sweat band and goggles. Unlike the rest of us, he doesn't own, and therefore plays without, a warmup suit, settling for shorts and a shirt instead. Dan's on-court comments are pretty much limited to "Over here!" and "Aw, rats!" The first phrase solicits a pass, the second punctuates a shot attempt. The frequency with which the phrases—uttered often and in pairs—occurred diminished as his teammates began to understand the pattern. Dan always has a knotted look, as though he thinks he may have left the stove on at home, or there's a stone in his shoe and he'll know what to do about it right after the game.

Roy. Roy is short and by far the best shot of the lot. He is also the baldest of the lot. I haven't determined if there's any correlation there, although at the proper angle in a well-lit room, he could blind a man of average height. Roy's enthusiasm is extreme by our standards but—as we have proved over many Sundays—not contagious. Of course, Roy makes at least 99% of his shots. He has perhaps keen eyesight, whereas the rest of us notice that our ardor for the game wanes as failing eyesight forces us to wait for *reports* of the outcome of our shots. Roy is hot.

Ed is not. But Ed doesn't care. I don't know where he was when the competitive genes were doled out or how he escaped being molded by American male myths, but Ed couldn't care less. Before and after games, he "strolls" up and down the court with a pipe, albeit unlighted, and talks and hums and encourages everybody. He looks as if he's playing the lead in *Going My Way*. Others of us stroll up and down the court as well—one of our rules is that you may not cross center court with the ball until all your teammates have crossed it. But none of us has the lilt in his step that Ed has, and no one has his "way to go, buddy" spirit. Ed cheers the guy who hits the basket that beats his team (when we keep score). Ed is the kind of guy who—without trying—reminds you that there's more to life than basketball, although while I'm playing I don't know what it might be.

On Sunday mornings in winter, basketball is my church. Joseph Campbell, the late educator, has reminded us that any religion works as long as we don't (or *it* doesn't) get stuck in its metaphors. I've been stuck in worse metaphors. Charlie is kind of stuck. He gets stuck opening his locker (he can't remember the combination). He gets stuck tying his shoelaces. Charlie is rather portly and when he gets down to floor level, it's the equivalent of a rain delay in baseball. We scream at him for taking so long, lecture him on the wonders of Velcro and then travel around him the next few trips up and down the court until he's up again.

He gets stuck when he shoots, too. Stuck to the floor. He uses a sort of jump shot with a lot of body motion. If you're not actually watching, you don't notice that his feet never leave the hardwood. Actually, Charlie isn't stuck, he just takes his time. He doesn't rush himself. He's at ease with himself. I think we all secretly envy him and would like to treat ourselves the way he treats himself. Like Ed, he smiles whether his shots go in or bounce out.

Back in the locker room Charlie is the one who powders Roy's head and says, "It's too bright on the court. Tone it down." Then Dan will say, "What was the score?" And Ed will say, "Ba-ba-ba-boo! Who knows?" And Dan will say, "Yeah, but who won?" And Roy will say, "I could use a Coke." And I will say, "I could use some Ben-Gay." And we shower and bewail our lack of hair, speed, vision and shot selection. Towel me off, dress me warmly. The steam rises off my head as I break into the cold morning air, leaving the gym and its metaphors. Leaving Charlie staring at his lock as if the right look will open it. Leaving Roy to his memories of knocking most all of them down, and Ed to the light of his pipe. For these and all thy blessings, we give thanks. And oh yeah, Dan, "We all won."

★   ★   ★

Originally appeared in *Sports Illustrated*, Vol. 71 # 26, December 18, 1989.

God is Hawaiian

When I die, I *hope* God is Hawaiian. After the lei is around my neck, and a clarifying hug, He, She, Source will step back, look into me, and in the beautiful and tender tradition of *Ho 'oponopono*, say,

"I'm sorry. . .

Please forgive me. . .

I love you. . .

Thank you. . ."

This is for all of us who are not Krishnamurti, whose mantra was, "I don't mind what happens." He sees I minded. Many times. He knows the "random" pain in His free design.

Then I too, will look into Him. Him. Most of what I viewed as horror and pain in the world was inflicted by males. And *I* say,

"I'm sorry. . .

Please forgive me. . .

I love you. . .

Thank you. . ."

This is for all the big and small misjudgments, narrowness, presumptions and arrogance I inflicted on Him, and on "the least of my brethren," who He kept telling me He was.

Then, in great clarity and light, He will summon all the luau people, and the Hula dancers, and Keola Beamer on slack key guitar, and say, "Get ready for a big one. This is my son. . . he's home. . . my son. . . in whom I am well pleased."

★ ★ ★

What I *suspect* will happen is that, in an instant, the Infinite in me, as me, will see, recognize, and know, in every sense, the Infinite as Source.

In either case it's Aloha.

For eternity. "O wow. . . O wow. . . O wow. . ."[18]

The years teach much which the days never knew.

Ralph Waldo Emerson

I Am. An Afterword

The two entries from my journal that I opened this book with, were two answers (at birth) to the question "Who am I?"

I'd like to close with a few reflections on who "I am" with no question marks.

Can I ever

be careful enough

in what I think

or say

or write,

can I ever

be careful enough

about what I put

after the words

"I am. . ."

Aren't most of the things I put after "I am" really more like "I feel?" I am mad. No. I *feel* mad. I am afraid. No. I feel afraid. Which also suggests a state. While I feel fear emphasizes transience. It comes and goes. And I *have feelings of fear* seems to name the most truth. All of it reminding us that *all words* have power and nuance, and all of them we use for self-talk especially, we would do well to pay attention to, and choose wisely.

The early Christian, first century mystics, those responsible for passing on the teachings of John, scribed, "In the beginning was the *Word*. And the Word *was* God." We had already been given the most precious pointer (in words) we have toward God. "I am that I am." It is the I am with nothing after it.

When I'm most "home" with my true Self, I experience the "Nothing" (no-thing) after the words. The I am that is beyond. Beyond description. Beyond naming. Beyond narrowing, capturing—in short, beyond the mind, wonderful as it is, that loves the *something* after everything, and how well it sizes it all up. Careful is not always its strong suit. Opening us to the Divine is not its job.

Pointing us in the right direction *can* be. And only the I Am can take us where it is only the I Am.

★   ★   ★

Some of my favorite pointer people and guides in this endless awakening.

With gratitude

> To Ramana Maharshi, for the gift of "Who Am I?" as a path.

> To Papagi and Robert Adams, his "students," for their flash of faceting.

> To Gangaji and Catherine Ingram, for wearing "shoes" like mine.

To Eckhart Tolle, for the childlike elegance and tools.

To Michael Singer, for the nuts-and-bolts-ness, along with such clear and present illustrations.

To Adyashanti, for his steadfast exploration of the naturalness and simplicity of awakening awareness.

To John Tarrant, for the mud coming up between the toes and all the secular sacraments.

To Hafiz, for reaching across six centuries to play with words and me.[19]

To Oprah, for Super Soul Sunday and all her beautiful world work.

And to Maleita, for daily getting "crazy" and "sane" with me, four feet in two "worlds."

Here's to unconditional joy.

And peace without cause.

Notes

1. These will be noted in the prequels to those pieces.

2. A light giving approach to anger, including as a path to awakening, is given by Gangaji in her book, *You Are That,* Volume II, chapter 5, Liberating Anger.

3. Omit if not an issue or after these subside.

4. My favorite exploration of, and approach to, meditation is found in Adyashanti's book, *True Meditation.*

5. Richard Melville Hall (Moby), from "We Are All Made of Stars."

6. Gerard Manley Hopkins, from "The World Is Charged With the Grandeur of God"(1877).

7. And now, of course, this book.

8. But the art supplies and fine brush fellows.

9. Since 1492 *the* standard in watercolor substrates.

10. Not, as before, serial choral groups.

11. From Wes Craven's film, *A Nightmare on Elm Street,* (1984).

12. Originated by Seena Frost. See www.soulcollage.com .

13. Available on itunes, at Amazon or www.giamusic.com .

14. See www.stephencovey.com . Used with permission

15. Critique or evaluation of your efforts.

16. Used with permission.

17. Now, of course, many such "leagues" exist, and our *President,* now past 50, is still an avid hoopster.

18. Steve Jobs.

19. So beautifully brought forth and contemporized by Daniel Ladinsky.

Also by Joe Wise

Albums:

Gonna Sing My Lord, 1966
Hand in Hand, 1968
A New Day, 1970
Sweet Water, 1970
Watch With Me, 1972
Welcome In, 1973
Take It For Gift, 1975
Take All the Lost Home, 1977
He Has Come, Songs for Christmas, 1977
Songs for the Journey, 1978
Lights of the City (with Ed Gutfreund and John Pell), 1979
And the Light Shines, 1982
Most Requested, Music for the Spirit, 1994
Most Requested, Music for the Spirit, Volume II , 2003

Children's Albums:

Close Your Eyes, 1974
Show Me Your Smile, 1976
Pockets, 1978
Doodle Bee Do, 1981
Don't Say Cheese, 1987

The Best of Joe Wise...Music for Kids, 1987
The Best of Joe Wise...Music for Kids Volume 2, 2003

Books:

The Body at Liturgy (no longer in print), 1972
Songprints, (a photo/poem essay), 1973
Through a Glass Lightly, (poems and essays), 1987
The Truth in Twenty, 2013★

Film Score:

A Time to Die, 1970

★This book available as paperback or e-book at <u>www. balboapress.com,</u> Amazon, Barnes and Noble, or from your local bookstore.

Most albums (as collections or single songs) and books, available at <u>www.giamusic.com</u>, itunes, and Amazon. The 2 *Most Requested* albums and the 2 *Best of Music for Kids* albums, as well as the *Pockets* album, are also available as CDs.

About the Author

Joe's music has been known and sung around the world since the mid 60's. His four degrees are in Philosophy, Theology, Education, and Counseling and Guidance. For the first 23 years of his work life he wrote music, recorded it and performed it; gave lectures, conducted workshops, and facilitated retreats—throughout the U.S. and Canada, as well as in Europe, Australia, and New Zealand.

Wise has been a resident of Arizona since 1995. Before that he lived 55 years in Louisville, Kentucky where between travels he offered a variety of workshops on writing and video story telling, including as facilitator with other artists at the Louisville Visual Artist Association and Bellarmine College.

His painting career has included studies with many accomplished artists including Ed Hermann and Joe Fettingis. His primary mentor was Dick Phillips. Joe is a member of the Sedona Visual Artists Coalition and a charter and juried member of the Northern Arizona Watercolor Society. His paintings have received numerous awards and hang in corporate headquarters and private collections.

He has written, produced, and recorded 22 albums of music, published 3 books and scored a film. He has worked for over a dozen years teaching writing as a therapeutic tool in treatment centers for addictions, and conducts retreats using the journal as a gateway for spiritual awareness and clarity. Joe lives with his wife Maleita in the Sedona area of Northern Arizona.

Joe can be contacted at: wise1@q.com
or through: www.joeandmaleitawise.com.

CPSIA information can be obtained at www.ICGtesting.com
Printed in the USA
BVOW08s2237230913

331897BV00002B/4/P